# MEET ME IN MANAGUA

*The Powerful Story of Nicaragua Reborn*

WENDY MURRAY ZOBA

**Photos by**
STEVE SONHEIM

Kregel Publications

*Meet Me in Managua: A Story of Nicaragua Reborn*

© 2005 by Wendy Murray Zoba
Photographs © 2005 by Steve Sonheim

Published by Kregel Publications, a division of Kregel, Inc., P.O. Box 2607, Grand Rapids, MI 49501.

All rights reserved. No part of this book may be reproduced, stored in a retrieval system, or transmitted in any form or by any means—electronic, mechanical, photocopy, recording, or otherwise—without written permission of the publisher, except for brief quotations in printed reviews.

Unless otherwise indicated, Scripture quotations are from the *Holy Bible, New Living Translation*, © 1996. Used by permission of Tyndale House Publishers, Inc., Wheaton, Illinois 60189. All rights reserved.

Scripture quotations marked NRSV are from the *New Revised Standard Version of the Bible*, © 1989 by the Division of Christian Education of the National Council of the Churches of Christ in the USA. Used by permission.

***Author's note:*** In part 4, I've preserved the words and diction of the Nicaraguan people. To some ears, it may seem odd, dissonant, or grammatically labored.

***Photographer's note:*** Photographs were taken during two trips to Nicaragua (fall 2003 and summer 2004). Photograph on page 126 by Jon Zoba.

ISBN 0-8254-4160-9

Printed in China

05 06 07 08 09 / 5 4 3 2 1

*For Tim*

*Poets! Towers of God*
*Made to resist the fury of the storms*
*Like cliffs beside the ocean*
*Or clouded, savage peaks!*
*Masters of lightning!*
*Breakwaters of eternity!*
*Hope, magic-voiced, foretells the day*
*When on the rock of harmony*
*The Siren traitorous shall die and pass away*
*And there shall only be*
*The full, frank-billowed music of the sea.*[1]
—RUBÉN DARÍO

CONTENTS

Acknowledgments . . . . . . . . . . . . . . . . . . . . . . . . . . . . . . . . . . .6
Introduction . . . . . . . . . . . . . . . . . . . . . . . . . . . . . . . . . . . . . . .9

## THE FIRST JOURNEY

### Part 1: Land of Poets
1. Quiet Stirrings . . . . . . . . . . . . . . . . . . . . . . . . . . . . . .15
2. A Fractious History . . . . . . . . . . . . . . . . . . . . . . . . .21
3. Betrayed Dreams . . . . . . . . . . . . . . . . . . . . . . . . . . .29

### Part 2: The Troubadour
4. Our Work Is Our Prayer . . . . . . . . . . . . . . . . . . . . .35
5. A Singing Bird . . . . . . . . . . . . . . . . . . . . . . . . . . . .43

### Part 3: Rhythms
6. Gathering the Pieces . . . . . . . . . . . . . . . . . . . . . . . .49
7. What It Takes to Build a Village . . . . . . . . . . . . . . .55

## THE SECOND JOURNEY

### Part 4: The Song
8. Ciudad Sandino . . . . . . . . . . . . . . . . . . . . . . . . . . .67
9. El Crucero . . . . . . . . . . . . . . . . . . . . . . . . . . . . . . .83
10. Nagarote . . . . . . . . . . . . . . . . . . . . . . . . . . . . . . . .91
11. San Ramón . . . . . . . . . . . . . . . . . . . . . . . . . . . . .107

Conclusion . . . . . . . . . . . . . . . . . . . . . . . . . . . . . . . . . .123
Endnotes . . . . . . . . . . . . . . . . . . . . . . . . . . . . . . . . . . .127

## ACKNOWLEDGMENTS

I wish to thank the following people for the encouragement and sustenance I needed to undertake and complete this project: Carla Sonheim, who conceived the project as a photo essay and who, in turn, fashioned the book; Jeff Crosby of InterVarsity Press for personally undertaking the advocacy of this project and getting it into the hands of Kregel; Dennis Hillman and Steve Barclift of Kregel for their gracious and persevering attendance to all aspects of this project; Randy Wittig for his helpful advice in its early stages; Alvaro Pereira, executive director of the American-Nicaraguan Foundation, who provided the vehicle *(el caballo)* and an excellent driver, José, who got me through those back roads to remote villages; Peter Schaller, Rainbow Network Director in Nicaragua, who masterfully orchestrated the interview schedule for my second trip as well as Steve Sonheim's follow-up photo sessions; Rainbow Network staff people, including Aura Lila Hernandez, Pedro Izaguirre, Jader Mejia, and Marilú Miranda Osegueda, who accompanied me to the corners of their respective communities to facilitate the interviews.

I wish to thank the John F. and Mary A. Geisse Foundation and the Rainbow Network and its board for making possible my trips to Nicaragua.

To the following individuals I bear special thanks: Steve Sonheim for sacrificing much to complete the photography for this book, bestowing beauty and dignity to the people of Nicaragua; Keith Jaspers for his gracious and accommodating attention to my every request; Marcos Rodriguez, my warrior-translator who literally walked each step with me along those dusty roads, and who became a beloved friend; Ali Geisse and Caroline Leibert, who brightened the second trip with their singing voices and enthusiasm; my beloved son Jon, who was a helper, a photographer, and the model of beatitude and humility on that trip; Tim Geisse, who introduced me to the work of Rainbow (and to Keith) and who helped carry the weight of this project with me at its every stage, without whom I could not have seen it to its end.

    I extend my arms in love to the people of Nicaragua, poets all, who opened their homes to me and told me their stories.

# INTRODUCTION

There were moments when I felt like I was taking crazy pills. During my trips to Nicaragua, to Missouri, and back again to Nicaragua, time and again I encountered situations that deviated from common rules. My son Ben, a college student in the East, sometimes writes e-mails with the subject line reading, *i feel like i'm taking crazy pills!...ja ja ja.* The "ja ja ja" denoting laughter, he writes the *h* of *ha ha* with a *j,* as is phonetically appropriate for Spanish speakers. *Crazy pills* refers to a line from a movie, Ben's comedic way of assimilating life's hardships and anomalies.

This undertaking emphasized the anomalies: a rich man, a poor country, a tired journalist, desperately poor and damaged people who embodied a picture of hope.

I learned about Keith Jaspers on my first trip to Nicaragua. He is the man who started an organization called Rainbow Network, an NGO (non-government organization). Given Nicaragua's history, that was the first anomaly—not the man, the NGO. Until little more than a decade ago there had never been a non-government anything related to Nicaragua's history. I was among a group who were driven around Managua and environs to see the countryside, to meet the people, to hear their stories about how Rainbow Network has touched their lives.

I witnessed a second contradiction the day I walked the crater lip of Volcán Masaya, some thirty kilometers south and east of Managua. When one climbs a mountain one expects to see life, to hear winds stirring, trees rustling, streams hurtling downward, riding gravity. "Everything on earth will worship you," the psalmist says, "they will sing your praises, shouting your name in glorious songs" (66:4). The earth doesn't begrudge declaring the handiwork of its Maker, so the desolation I saw induced a mild shock. Instead of vivacity I found charred ridges, lifeless knotty trees, and a yawning volcano cavity belching toxins from the bowels of a mountain. The Spanish called it the gateway to hell. They raised a cross high on an overlook to slake hell's fire and bless the mountain, to hold high a promise.

I felt overwhelmed by the quiet. Only the crunching of stones beneath my feet signaled the presence of life. It was a desolate landscape—dust and pumice and tree skeletons and dry grass. It seemed a picture of what wars can do to the spirit of a people—the damage and desolation that can overtake a conquered—or in any case trampled—nation. Then appeared another contradiction: a bright yellow bird—a *chocayos del crater*, crater parakeet—alighted in a barren tree. Defying theories of science and survival, this curious bird sustains life there, notwithstanding the toxins of that crater. One might call it a miracle, a spirited assertion of life amid "inhospitable conditions." For that fleeting moment, beauty and desolation found each other—a picture of improbabilities.

And so with thoughts about desolation and wars, I have written a book about Nicaragua's peace. I found the story in the work of an NGO. The term is bland. It doesn't do service to the hope that arises in the Nicaraguan imagination upon hearing the word "rainbow." So I've called it a story of rebirth: a tale of revolution and dreams; of betrayal and new hope; about being lost, and then found.

On one level it's the story of a fair-haired, ruddy-faced Missourian who alighted in Nicaragua like a bright bird on the ridge of smoldering rock, Keith Jaspers, a self-made entrepreneur who decided to share his wealth. Getting to know him, however, I came to understand he could be any man or woman with a dream and the willingness to step inside it. He called his dream "Rainbow" because of the promise it carries. In this destitute, war-torn, misery-fatigued, one-time Marxist nation, Keith has managed to impart business *savoir-faire* and American-dream gusto into the aspirations of the people. Raising chickens to sell eggs here feels like winning the lottery.

Nicaragua's national history is charted by pre-Colombian intertribal rivalries, Spanish domination, invasions and occupations, the reign of cruel tyrants, and insurgence of rebels. Let us note, too, that Nicaragua's history is inextricably linked to and tinged with antipathy toward the policies of foreign governments, including those of the United States.

The small country would defy the shame of foreign imposition, even if it meant war, which it did time and again. Nicaraguans claimed self-determination of a kind, though they paid for it dearly. Their history has bequeathed scars to its people who've been terrorized by cruel dictators; driven to take up arms in revolt against them; disillusioned by the failures and betrayals of their revolutionary deliverers; traumatized by seemingly endless *guerrilla* conflicts in its highlands, neighbor against neighbor—many, I learned, resulting from policies of the U.S. government.

Nicaragua has been misunderstood. Some call it the "black sheep" of Central America because its name invokes images of AK-47s, soldiers in berets, journalists shot point-blank in the head, muddy green uniforms, face paint, and fists raised in defiance. In 1990 the struggling nation rallied its grassroots base to unify and bury their arms. That year Nicaragua held free elections. The rebuilding groped forward while the wars, raised fists, face paint, and related conflicts faded from view. Then Hurricane Mitch hit in 1998. Their hardships have made me wonder what it takes for the average Nicaraguan to get out of bed in the morning.

Walking the high ridge of Volcán Masaya, I pondered losses and damaged lives and possibilities and new hope. There were moments I could utter only a mystified *ja ja ja*. In all my travels, stateside and in Central America, I encountered strange yearnings and poignant, crushing moments written in the faces of the people I met. I was to chase these elusive feelings, or maybe they were chasing me, until in the end, I caught them—or they caught me—by the conclusion of this assignment.

When I met the people of Nicaragua, I was not able to know what it took for them to get out of bed those mornings. I know only that when I came, they painted pictures and hung palm fronds over archways; they did little dances and sang happy songs; from their souls I heard poetry.

> *A friend crossed my path*
> *and gave me his hand.*
> *He came from far away and*
> *Gave life to my dreams.*[1]

Is there life beneath the smoldering rock? Is there a promise held high? Can a bright, singing bird summon it? The answer lies in the song God is singing in the hearts of the Nicaraguan people.

# The First Journey

*God is alive. Go ahead, translate that.*

—Keith Jaspers

# Part I
## *Land of Poets*

### 1
### QUIET STIRRINGS

Keith wore the same cotton plaid shirt he'd worn on and off all week, along with a baseball cap just off his brow. During my first trip, three of us—Keith Jaspers, Rainbow board member, my good friend Tim Geisse, and I—had remained in Managua after the rest of the group had left. Tim and I stayed an extra day to help Keith interview on camera Nicaraguans at Rainbow's main office in the neighborhood called Ciudad Sandino. Tim, a lawyer in Cleveland, wore tennis shoes and travel shorts and a Piggly-Wiggly T-shirt. He operated the video camera, that is, when he wasn't fussing with the shelves behind to neaten the background. Keith clutched a small tape recorder for back-up audio recordings and his personal color commentary. I curled up in a chair in a corner, pen and notebook in hand, rallying from sickness that had overtaken me that morning. There were no windows in the room and we didn't run fans because they'd create background noise. Sweat poured out of us.

The first visitor, a young man in a wheelchair, rolled himself in. On his lap sat a baby boy. The child's eyes sparkled like diamonds and he was crowned with a bright knitted cap. The man said his name was Jairro Sarivia, twenty-four, father of two with a wife nineteen years old. He had come to thank Mister Keith for the wheelchair Rainbow had given to him.

He explained he'd been riding a bike to his sister's funeral when "a car passed and ran over me." He said, "Since that day I can't walk."

I thought, *Wait a minute. Your sister's funeral?*

"Before, I was normal and I could walk," he said. "I have accepted my situation, though it is bad and terrible. My legs will never walk. I am a young person. I have things to do for my sons. I have problems. But I want to continue with my future. I say thanks to God who is big, and who we ask for protection."

Keith said, "I want you in the microloan program. You can do stuff in that wheelchair. Leonardo [a Rainbow staff worker], please help him do this." Leonardo nodded. Jairro Sarivia smiled shyly and retreated, turning his chair, his baby's fat fists bobbing.

Manuel Rorozco shuffled in next. He smiled under a handlebar mustache. Keith handed me a microtape. "Label this one 'tape two.'"

We learned that Manuel had successfully used a micro business loan to establish needed competition in his neighborhood. "Before there was only one little store and it was very expensive," he said. "With my loan I could set up a little store in my house."

Keith interrupted. "Bring back Jairro. I want him to hear this." Leonardo promptly exited and in a moment returned with Jairro, the baby happy as a clam on his lap.

Manuel repeated his story for Jairro. "I had a loan of two thousand cordobas," he said. "In four months I had nineteen hundred cordobas in profit. I will be taking out a second loan of two thousand cordobas to buy more products for my store—sugar, rice, beans, corn, candies. The other store sold a pound of rice for four cordobas. I sell mine for three."

Keith asked Manuel if he could help Jairro do the same thing.

The two lived too far apart for that to happen, it turned out. Keith asked Manuel if this was something he'd been praying for. Manuel said, "I believe God answers anybody who requests of him. If the community wouldn't make any prayers, there wouldn't be any answers."

Thus, my first glimpse of the work of Rainbow Network included a list of improbable characters—a millionaire in a ball cap shuffling microtapes and micromanaging rice and bean networks; a Piggly-Wiggly bedecked lawyer mastering camera angles; a baby drooling onto the floor; two Nicaraguans giving praises with shining eyes, one of whom lost the ability to walk while traveling a road to bury his sister.

This picture did not fit my earliest impression of Nicaragua.

❖ ❖

During the summer of 1979 while pregnant with my first baby, I turned on the evening news and saw a man on his knees. Another man, a smaller man wearing boots and military fatigues, stood over him, holding a gun. I'd missed the warning that attended the clip—*What you are about to see may not be appropriate for young viewers.* Before I knew what I was looking at, the uniformed man raised the gun and aimed its muzzle at the head of the kneeling man, who lurched and fell dead—right there on the evening news.

I wondered what kind of world my child would be born into. The name associated with the killing had been "Somoza" and the country, Nicaragua. I thought Somoza a deplorable man and Nicaragua an appalling country. I vowed then if I heard the missionary call I'd defy the heavens before I'd go to Central America, which is where I ended up almost ten years later.

From 1990 to 1994 I lived in Honduras, a country closely linked to Nicaragua's history, but anyway, *not there*. I traveled throughout Central America in those years, mostly west, to El Salvador and Guatemala, a brief stop in Belize. I shed my U.S.-coddled sensibilities and attained the thick skin that grows on expatriates living in third-world countries. Even still, the horror of that news clip never left me. In all my travels, I didn't go east, to that unwelcoming place where helpless men get shot in the head.

❖ ❖

Now I was in the land that had once seemed so forbidding, having been invited by Keith to travel there in March 2003. I was confounded, then, when strange affections I could not explain arose in me, first when Tim Geisse and I were driving along volcano roads and, later, sitting for hours in the back of the van chatting with our translator, Marcos Rodriguez. He had been a Sandinista soldier who fought Contras four years in the mountains we were then traversing. We were both lovers of language and during those long rides we traded idioms. I taught him regional expressions for the second person plural: *"You guys. Y'all. Yons. Youse."* He taught me *"tras cuernos palos":* disgrace comes over and over again from different places.

Maybe it was driving along volcano ridges that stirred those yearnings. Maybe it had been Marcos's gentle demeanor, a man of thirty-seven, husband and father, former border guard who'd confessed to still trembling in fear of being ambushed as we drove mountain roads. Maybe it was the mountains themselves, festooned in palms and laurels and acacias and mango trees. Maybe it was Marcos's being a dead ringer for Billy Crystal, I don't know. These were simple moments. Yet quiet stirrings arose within me.

At one point in the journey, it occurred to me that Nicaragua might best be understood as a nation of poets. I later learned that author Mario Vargas Llosa had said, "Nicaraguans have a natural urge for poetry." Nicaragua's favored son is, in fact, the acclaimed poet Rubén Darío (1867–1916). When this country is seen as a nation of poets, everything makes sense: the invasions and revolts, the heroic last stands, the raised AK-47s of the revolution, the Contra insurgence—counter-revolutionaries against revolutionaries. Poetic cadence spills even from the names of its champions—heroes and villains: Sandino, Chamorro, Obando, Castro, Darío, Fonseca, Somoza, Ortega.

Plate tectonics—the movement of the earth's under parts—is the key to understanding volcanoes, and it is also the key to understanding Nicaragua. Earth's rhythms rise beneath the feet of its people. Over there a mountain smokes. Over here a mountain waits. The land is a power that must be reckoned with.

Don Quixote asked his luckless escort Sancho as they wandered in the night:

"How can you, Sancho, see . . . when the night is so dark that not a single star appears in the sky?"

"Yes, that is true," said Sancho, "but fear has many eyes and sees things underground and much more in the sky."

Nicaraguans' eyes, like Sancho's, see underground and see much more in the sky. Theirs has been a story of fear, but always tempered with dreams. That is why I see Nicaragua as a nation of poets. For a poet "lives on the bridge between the world's contradiction and the soul's imperishable dream."[1] Despair and hope rise and retreat in the landscape of the Nicaraguan heart. It feels the earth's movements. Steam rises soft beneath their feet. They see painted sunsets that hold the promise of a dream. Hidden behind sunsets people like Jairro Sarivia and Manuel Rorozea see colors of a rainbow.

## 2
## A FRACTIOUS HISTORY

We traveled to Nicaragua's coffee-growing northern highlands, the land where Marcos, the translator, still trembled. There, we stopped at an abandoned coffee farm that had been converted to a sewing school. We parked below and scaled a mountain path on foot to reach it. Passing an old warehouse on our right, we couldn't miss the brightly painted mural on its outer wall. Revolutionary icon Che Guevara hailed us, and behind his image, in darker tones, stood the shadow of Augusto César Sandino, Nicaragua's revolutionary conscience and mythic hero.

Atop the embankment, girls at the school greeted us with a dance. They were pretty little birds with turtledove eyes and bows in their hair. They wiggled their hips in ruffled dresses and twirled like butterflies in flight. In sweet voices they delivered a poem while Marcos translated. Captivated by little lassies pirouetting on the shoulders of a shadowy Sandino, I scribbled as fast as I could, but missed more than I caught. A moment later, I elbowed him, asking what the little girls had said in their poem. He answered, "I don't know. I was translating."

As noted, the history of this young democracy is wrought with revolutions, incursions, champions, and villains too convoluted to try and make sense of it here. Even so, some history must be underscored in order to grasp the present-day consciousness of Nicaraguan spirit. (I will do my best to find the right balance.)

The country's first inhabitants were shell-gatherers known as *Los Concheros,* a Carib people who inhabited the eastern Atlantic coastline eight thousand years ago. An agriculture-based civilization soon followed, and with it the cultivation of sacred corn that typifies all Mesoamerica. The overpowering Aztecs arose in Mexico in the thirteenth century and drove to the east the Chorotega and Nicarao peoples, who settled the land of a great lake and smoking mountains. Caribs and Miskito Indians dwelt along the Atlantic coast and, for a time, remained isolated. Expansion and politics inevitably found them out.

Cristobel Colón encountered Nicaragua's native peoples on his final trip to the Americas in 1502. He skirted the Miskito Coast, taking back gold and parrots and women. He left word with fellow adventurers of the existence of "the best land and people that we've found in the New World."[1] So the conquest began. In 1523 *los conquistadores* Gil Gonzales Dávila and Andres Niño marched up from Panama, defeated tribal leaders, and took the towns of Granada, Léon, and Masaya, claiming Nicaragua for Spain. (Their inability to render Indian names properly explains the present pronunciation of some towns: *Nahualotli* became Nagarote; *Manahuac*, Managua; *Matlalcapan*, Matagalpa.)

In the late 1500s, holding off a would-be takeover by British pirates, Nicaragua joined the Captaincy General of Guatemala to enhance their protection. In 1821, with its Central American neighbors, Nicaragua won independence from Spain and established itself as the Republic of Nicaragua in 1838.

Disputes and local rivalries erupted over the decades that followed. Leadership emerged from wealthy families from the two key power centers, Léon ("liberal") and Granada ("conservative").[2] The United States at this time was seeking a place to develop an inter-oceanic canal and had commissioned Nashvillian adventurer, William Walker, to search for possibilities in Nicaragua. Walker fell in with leaders in Léon. In a Quixote-esque flourish, he stormed and conquered rival Granada with an army of three hundred. Two years later (1856) he declared himself president.

Walker's bravado personified Nicaragua's worst nightmares about foreign interests imposing themselves (especially the U.S.). Walker's ambition gave rise to a rare occasion of solidarity between these otherwise fractious liberal and conservative parties, and they defeated him in September 1856. The U.S. withdrew from Nicaragua in 1857. Walker was captured and executed three years later during a similar campaign in Honduras.

For the next fifty years Nicaragua's history followed the script that defined most Central American nations: The rich governed the poor; the rich got richer while the poor got poorer. Granada-based conservatives ruled for decades thereafter, liberals having been disgraced by their ties with Walker. Under their watch care, however, much land went to U.S.-owned lumber companies and coffee growers, elbowing out the peasant farmers.

Over the years the U.S. oversaw the imposition of conservative leaders who yielded access to Nicaragua's abundant natural resources. Under the reign of puppet-president Adolfo Díaz, discontentment reached critical levels. Revolutionary enthusiasm surged under the leadership of teacher and judge Benjamin Zeledón, who vowed to fight to the death the "traitor" Díaz, who met the terms. He requested U.S. marines to slake the fires of revolt. As marines stormed Zeledón's position in the last rebel holdout, he wrote his wife: "I have no illusions. By taking up the rifle and refusing the humiliating offers of money and honors made to me, I signed my own death warrant. But if that sentence is carried out I will die serenely, because each drop of my blood spilled in defense of the nation and its freedom will give life to a hundred Nicaraguans who, like me, will take up arms against the betrayal of our beautiful but unfortunate Nicaragua."[3] He died in August of 1912. U.S. occupation of Nicaragua began that year, and would last another twenty-plus. Local legend says that on the streets of Masaya a young man stood and watched, outraged to see Díaz's troops kick and desecrate the lifeless body of Benjamin Zeledón. That young man was Augusto César Sandino.

❖ ❖

Sandino is a name fraught with mystery and pathos for Nicaraguans, the man from whom the Sandinistas derived their name. He was the illegitimate son of a peasant woman and a wealthy judge who'd abandoned them both to live his respectable life with a wife and legitimate heirs. Sandino carried dreams for his beloved Nicaragua, and his dreams became their dreams. He called into question the way of life that would allow his mother to be jailed for failing to pay a debt, while his wealthy father carried on without consequence or thought of her plight. Young Sandino cared for his mother while she was in prison, and the injustices in her life riled him, as did all the inequities that were carried on the backs of all of Nicaragua's poor.

In 1921 he had to flee his beloved Nicaragua when a political debate ended in his stabbing his antagonist. He landed in Mexico where he became enamored with the sentiments of union organizers who denounced American dominance in Mexican oil fields. He wrote,

> I felt deeply hurt when they called me a shameless traitor who had allowed his country to be bought and sold. At first I resisted those accusations, saying that since I was not a man of state, I did not deserve them. But later I reflected more deeply, and I came to understand that they were right, since I was a Nicaraguan and had a right to protest. . . .
>
> About 1925 I decided everything in Nicaragua had gone sour and that honor had disappeared. At the same time my sincerity attracted a group of like-minded friends. Each day we would comment on the submission of our people before the advance, by treachery or force, of Yankee imperialism. On one such day I said to my friends, if there were 100 honorable men who loved their country as I did, our nation could recover its absolute sovereignty stolen from us by the Yankee empire.[4]

Sandino returned to Nicaragua in 1926 and rallied a band of several hundred "honorable" but disgruntled mine workers in the Segovia hills at San Rafael del Norte. From there he launched a six-year military campaign that indelibly marked the Nicaraguan consciousness. In 1927 Sandino and his guerrilla fighters carried out an impressive fifteen-hour assault on the U.S. marine base at Ocotal. They nearly defeated them save for a contingency he hadn't anticipated: air power. U.S. planes appeared and dropped shells that wiped out nearby villages.

Sandino was forced to retreat. For the next five years he stymied all attempts of the U.S. Marines to flush him out of mountain jungles and chose his ambush targets strategically. After swift and random attacks he'd disappear into the hills and evade capture, which only enhanced his mystique. Facing political opposition and economic hardship at home, and increasing frustration over Sandino's humiliations, President Herbert Hoover made the stunning decision in 1932 to withdraw the marines from Nicaragua. The man in the shadows with his modest band of rebels at long last drove foreign interests off Nicaraguan soil.

❖ ❖

Back in the van, having departed the sewing school, we were traveling through downtown Matagalpa, and Marcos and I had resumed our discussion of idioms. I was explaining *down pat*. "It's when you are in command of something," I said. "It's under your control. You've got it *down pat*." Tim honked. I looked out the window in time to see a helpless dog squirm under the wheel of an oncoming bus. Many of us gasped. The bus that had hit the dog didn't stop. I looked again and saw the dog lifeless on the road, turning to Marcos, horrified. His ear slightly cocked, he awaited further explanation—not of the dead dog, but of *down pat*. Marcos had served in the Sandinista army four years (1984–88) and arose each morning during those years as he had arisen during the days of Somoza's terror campaigns. "I realized my brothers were gone and that I was going to die the way my friends got killed." The sight of a dog dead on the street did not alarm him.

The reign of terror that scarred the lives of Nicaraguans like Marcos commenced with the departure of U.S. marines from Nicaragua in 1932. At that time the marines installed a general named Anastasio Somoza García as commander of the newly created military force called the National Guard. In early 1933, while Augusto Sandino traveled to Managua for peace talks and to attend a banquet at the presidential palace, he was ambushed and assassinated by Somoza's national guardsmen at the orders of *El Generál Somoza*.

After Sandino's assassination in 1934 the guerrilla movement he'd launched "went to sleep for a while," Marcos said, while Somoza, empowered by the National Guard, emerged *en force*. He drove the enfeebled President Sacasa from office. By 1937 Somoza had suspended the constitution and seized control of the country, commencing a forty-year dynastic reign of brutality and fraud. The first Somoza was assassinated in September 1956. His son, Luis Somoza Debayle, succeeded him and ruled six years before deferring in 1963 to his younger brother Anastasio, known as Tachito.

"All of them were nasty," Marcos said. "They all oppressed and exploited the people. But Tachito was the worst. He became rich with properties of peasant farmers he forced to leave their lands."

During the sixties and seventies, the third Somoza made "profitable" investments in gambling, drug smuggling, and prostitution to top off the railroads, factories, steam ship lines, lumber companies, and breweries he'd hijacked. "He became very rich when the earthquake hit in 1972," said Marcos. "Donations and money coming from abroad were channeled to his pockets. The earthquake was a great opportunity for Tachito to get richer." By the mid-seventies his estimated worth was about a billion dollars.

"Every year the people were seeing more cruelty and were developing the feeling of rejection toward Somoza," Marcos said. "The Sandinistas got organized to fight the Somoza regime and overthrow the dictatorship."

The spirit of Sandino rose again. In the early 1960s, guerrilla insurgents reorganized. Cuba's insurrection was their model and Fidel Castro, in the eyes of many Nicaraguans, had assumed the heroic stature of Sandino. Their goal was the violent overthrow of Somoza and purgation of all remnants of "Yankee imperialism." The newly formed FSLN *(Frente Sandinista de Liberación Nacionál)*, funded by the Soviets, trained by the Cubans, and warmly allied with the PLO, implanted their guerrilla bands in the mountains. "Mountain warfare was a way for them to hide themselves," said Marcos. "There were alternatives and opportunities there." They undertook random campaigns against National Guard outposts throughout the 1960s, but claimed little in the way of military successes.

Over time, as Somoza's cruelties persisted, the FSLN gained grassroots support. "Somoza's National Guard were in the countryside killing people they thought were sympathetic with the Sandinistas," said Marcos. "They were killing innocent people. Both in the mountains and in the cities, Somoza would send troops to fight the Sandinista guerrillas. Many very strong battles took place in these mountains."

Fractious infighting among the rebels threatened to dissolve gains made by the revolutionaries, so Castro used his charisma and authority to demand unity for the cause. For the next fifteen years the Sandinistas waged a vigorous guerrilla campaign against the Somoza regime and the Nicaraguan people rallied around their deliverers to the path of liberation.

## 3
## BETRAYED DREAMS

Our road-weary group made a final stop that long day at a grassy plain under the shadow of Volcán Momotombo. At that stop Rainbow was dedicating land they'd planned to build houses upon, to start a community. Nicaraguans had gathered from surrounding neighborhoods and we stood in a circle, hats lifted and heads lowered to pray. Momotombo stood in the background, the sun's late rays painting it purple and orange. Grasses stirred and trees rustled in the wind. Children dashed about the field grabbing balloons. "Thank you for husbands and families," someone prayed. I thought, *Some day soon this ground will be home to these children. A community will rise here.*

I recalled earlier that day, sitting in the van as Marcos told me the story of his youth, which meant the story of Somoza's terror and the subsequent revolution. I'd been astounded that a country of four million peasants could figure a way to say "no more" and overthrow their U.S.-backed dictator.

❖ ❖

Marcos had described how the Sandinistas had gained terrain and popularity over the long years under Somoza's brutality. Through pamphlets and the underground Radio Sandino, they'd kept the population abreast of guerrilla movements. Their first attempt at liberation took place in September 1978, when Marcos was twelve. "There were uprisings, but Somoza had very strong weapons," he said. The attempt failed and the National Guard became more aggressive. "Between September 1978 and July 1979 the National Guard were killing a lot of youth, bombing cities, and doing bad things," said Marcos. "They would go to a neighborhood and kill any young people found in the street. Almost every day we had four, or five, or six, or ten young people killed. I remember a time in my town of Léon when young people were gathered in one of the churches. The National Guard ran in and killed the people right there in the church. They didn't have weapons. You could hear everything. We hid in our houses. The last month of the Somoza regime there were many violent killings and battles. I saw it as a young man. It was a horrible situation."

The shocking ruthless killing on June 20, 1979, of American broadcast journalist Bill Stewart brought Somoza's teetering reign to its final collapse. Those traveling with Stewart convinced the agitated guardsmen who'd witnessed the killing that they would turn a blind eye, and so were allowed to go. What the guardsmen hadn't realized was that Stewart's cameraman had perched his camera on the dashboard of the jeep and caught the whole thing on tape. This was the clip I saw that day in June, the summer of my first pregnancy. It turns out the entire civilized world reacted with the same horror I did. Somoza knew his days were numbered. "After that most of the people in Nicaragua both in the cities and the countryside got organized and said, 'We're going to overthrow Somoza, that's what is going to happen.' And that happened."

Standing now on that grassy field, the sun casting long shadows, I caught a vision of a young man on a street where life's themes played out in black and red—guns and the blood of fallen heroes. Augusto Sandino wrote once, "They made fun of Nicaraguans in the rest of the world," and I thought of the idiom Marcos had taught me: *"tras cuernos palos"*—disgrace comes over and over again from different places. I thought of Sandino's mother, who got lost in the story, a slave, and crushed under forces that demeaned her.

Marcos had said Somoza's last gasps were marked by "airplanes throwing bombs over the city." The National Guard had fled their headquarters. Somoza took refuge in Paraguay. July 19, 1979, was the day of the victory of the Revolution. "On that day all the people got together on La Plaza de La Revolución in Managua. Sandinista guerrillas came from north and south and east and west," Marcos said. "Thousands of people waited for their heroes from all over Nicaragua to celebrate the triumph of the Revolution."

The Sandinista leadership were idealists. It turned out they understood more about vilifying Yankee imperialism than reviving a battle-weary damaged country. At the time of the overthrow, it was estimated Somoza owned sixty-five percent of the land (his friends and supporters much of the rest). Sandinista leadership confiscated the properties and redistributed the land to peasant farmers, which proved only minimally successful. First, "the people didn't care about the land because they didn't have to pay anything for it and didn't take good care of it," Marcos said. Second, the government neglected to teach these peasants how to run and maintain the equipment. The majority of redistributed properties ended up in ruin. "Many, many farms failed. The poor became poorer again."

Some other attempts of the fledgling government however did manage to "raise up the people," as Marcos put it. A vigorous vaccination campaign eradicated polio, and "women, youth, peasant farmers, and workers in the city got organized," he said. "There were many organizations in Nicaragua."

The Sandinistas could rightly claim a stunning victory in ousting the defiant Somoza. Unwilling to give ground to forces they'd struggled so fiercely to overcome, the new government clung tenaciously to the spirit of revolution. What they failed to see, however, was that what "raised up the people" was not a commitment to an ideology so much as hope for better days.

Farms were failing. "Organizations" didn't feed starving families. Discontentment fueled by disenchantment began to stir. The Sandinistas found themselves in the vexing if not self-contradictory position of having to *impose* the revolutionary spirit. The same tactics of terror and coercion availed by Somoza to quench fires of revolt, became useful to the Sandinistas to prop it up.

In any case, events beyond their borders conspired to alter the landscape of history. Ronald Reagan became U.S. president in 1981, and he didn't look kindly

upon Marxist-Leninist revolutions. Through the CIA, the United States set up military camps along the Honduras-Nicaragua border to train and equip counter-revolutionary Nicaraguans (dispossessed Somoza supporters), called Contras, to fight Sandinistas on their own turf and with their own rules of war.

The Sandinistas responded with muscle. By 1983 the government had imposed forced inscription of Nicaraguan youths, implemented in 1984, which "the people didn't like at all," Marcos said. "Years were passing and more people were getting killed in the mountains. There was a food shortage because of the U.S. embargo. There was a war going on. The people did not know what to do. The people were in despair. They developed hatred toward the Sandinistas. There wasn't a revolution anymore. They didn't want to talk about peace with the counter-revolutionaries. Mothers hated to have their sons being killed in the mountains. The Sandinistas would bring them in the coffin and say, 'This is your son,' and that's it. Mothers were crying and were developing hatred against the Sandinistas. Many times mothers would open the coffin and there wasn't any corpse inside. There was a banana tree. They said, 'This is your son,' and it was a tree trunk.

"That is why many people joined the contra army." Over the years the Contras gained strength the same way followers of Sandino once had, as more people rallied to fight the Sandinistas whom they felt had betrayed the revolution. "The people didn't want the Contras back in power because it reminded them of the National Guard," said Marcos. "They were saying they are against the Sandinistas."

"Peace is a process. It's an outlook, a way to live," said Costa Rica's President Oscar Arias, who won the Nobel Peace Prize for his efforts that finally resulted in peace, in 1988, for his neighboring country. "You can never say that hopes for peace are lost. Peace is always waiting for us. Dialogue is the only way to resolve problems. Sooner or later, even Nicaraguans recognize that."[1]

❖ ❖

Shadows fell on Momotombo. Someone prayed, *People will belong to each other, husbands to wives, children to parents, neighbors to each other.* I thought of little girls in white dresses waving dainty arms and speaking poems in sweet voices. "I learned so many good things from my time in the military," Marcos had said of those many years defined by death. "It was part of my integrated education. I learned about solidarity, the value of my family, my friends, how I want to share what I have." Sandino had lamented that the rest of the world made fun of Nicaraguans, that "disgrace came over and over again from different places." "My country . . . was in such need of love from its people," he'd said. Maybe the rage and ferocity and courage that burned in his heart was really his attempt to see his mother in a ruffled dress, arms floating like a butterfly. Maybe he was a poet and was remembering his mother when he wrote those words about his beloved Nicaragua needing love from its people. Maybe his poem got lost, the way the words of the little girls' poem got lost when Marcos couldn't repeat them, fixed as he was on "translating" them. Maybe the message behind the jungle hideouts and ambushes and slit throats was really the cry of a poet for something more powerful than revolution.

Marcos went back to those little girls and learned the words to that poem:

> *Look at my little hands*
> *how clean they are.*
> *I'm going to wash them*
> *with a little soap.*
> *Now I am ready to greet you.*

Keith Jaspers

# Part II
## *The Troubadour*

### 4
### OUR WORK IS OUR PRAYER

Now we return to the image of the ruddy-faced Missourian, Keith Jaspers, whom I had come to know during that first trip to Nicaragua. (One gets to know people you travel third-world roads with.) A tallish man with red hair and an impish grin, Keith was the inspiration that rose us from our beds at dawn every morning, sleep or no sleep, the way a tornado inspires one to run. He'd indulge us a lingering second cup of coffee at breakfast, but only just. Then it would be, "Come on, people, we need to roll." How many times had I heard that voice telling us it was time to roll?

One of the mornings on that first trip, over that—in my case—third cup of coffee, Keith led a brief devotion. He wanted us to understand why people associated with Rainbow poured such time, energy, travel, money, and human fortitude into the work in Nicaragua. "It comes out of Matthew 25," he said. "I can't remember what verse."

His son Steve interjected: "Forty." Steve Jaspers was numbered among our group, the youngest of the three Jaspers offspring and only male. He managed the Wingate Inn near St. Louis. He pulled out his Palm Pilot, found the verse in Matthew 25 and read it aloud: "And the king will answer them, 'Truly I tell you, just as you did it to one of the least of these who are members of my family, you did it to me.' Then he will say to those at his left hand, 'You that are accursed, depart from me into the eternal fire prepared for the devil and his angels; for I was hungry and you gave me no food, I was thirsty and you gave me nothing to drink, . . . these will go away into eternal punishment, but the righteous in eternal life'" (vv. 40–42, 46 NRSV).

Keith interrupted. "That's the part that scares me, the separating them out part."

Before we "rolled" that day, shuffling backpacks and grabbing water bottles, Keith said, "I like to quote Mother Teresa: 'The poor are Jesus in his most distressing disguise.' She said, 'You pray the work by doing it.' That's what our organization is about. Our work is our prayer."

The Keith Jaspers I came to know on that trip abounded in color commentary. At every turn, he'd rehearse Nicaragua's history and social demographics; Rainbow's efforts, needs, accomplishments, and deficits; people's maladies and dreams; and Mother Teresa's adages, all in a relentless commitment to keeping—I'll rephrase that—trying to keep the schedule. "Dad wouldn't have raised hogs in a building like this," he'd said, referring to a shack we visited with a dilapidated roof held on by rocks. The only "bed" in it serviced a family of five, one of the families that would soon move to a new concrete block home up the road as participants in a Rainbow housing project. Keith had said, pointing to the shack (echoing a sermon of his friend Anthony Campolo about the day Jesus died), "This is Friday. Over there"—he pointed up the road where we'd later attend the housing project dedication ceremony, "That's Sunday." He'd said, "Never in their wildest dreams did these people believe they'd live in a home with a cement floor and a metal roof."

The Keith I came to know on that first trip lavished encouragement on the Nicaraguan people, along with no small measure of corny wit. We'd visited the rural community of El Socorro and he said to the children: "I heard a rumor in Managua the most beautiful children in Nicaragua live in El Socorro." To a 19-year-old scholarship student in the village of Trinidad Central, he said, "You're an intelligent young man and you attract all these pretty girls to the school." Farther down the road at a Rainbow feeding center in El Carmen, community volunteers told him that this and other feeding centers in the area fed "418 children, 65 pregnant women, 65 nursing women, 248 old people, and 44 special cases," to which Keith responded, "And I know every one of them by name."

. . . "There is a rumor that the most beautiful children in Nicaragua live in El Carmen. Is it true?"

. . . "Saddle up people, let's go."

. . . "Did anybody see the face of Jesus today?"

The Keith Jaspers I came to know a month later, on his home turf of Springfield, Missouri, in some ways surprised me. He and his wife Karen are wealthy self-made entrepreneurs, jointly owning (with their three children) three hotels in Branson and another in St. Louis. The home they inhabit is beyond the reach of the wildest dream of any Nicaraguan.

Coming into Springfield that day in early May, clouds blanketed the sky with random breaks hurling sunlight over meadows and hills of the Ozarks. For all the places I'd been in the world, I'd never been there. You can't call them mountains really. And as hills they don't command the astonishment of volcanoes. Even so, upholding the spirit of the Heartland, these rugged cliffs of layered limestone and clay seemed content to be a footstool to welcome the traveler.

Knowing Keith as I thought I did, it was no surprise upon my arrival at the Jaspers Family Hotels headquarters to find in his office an eclectic mix of Nicaraguan kitsch and wheeler-dealer business appurtenances. Here was a Nicaraguan pencil holder. There was a photograph of Keith and Karen with the Gephardts. On the shelf near the Nicaragua-shaped clock were photos of Keith and Karen with Al Gore, and Keith and Karen with Bob Hope. Up and over a bit hung a trowel in a frame honoring his twelve years of service on the board of Habitat for Humanity. Over yon, the Cendant Hotel Division Humanitarian Award was displayed next to the Howard Johnson Humanitarian Award. The books on his shelf were no less diverse: *Essential Spanish*, *The Theology of the Hammer* (Millard Fuller), *Miracles* (C.S. Lewis), *In His Steps* (Charles Sheldon), *Sources of Strength* (Jimmy Carter), and three *New Testaments* (Revised Standard Version). On the opposite wall Norman Rockwell's "The Golden Rule" held forth, a replica of a

*Saturday Evening Post* cover that read "Do unto Others as You Would Have Them Do unto You." On the wall by the window hung a calendar with trains.

We chatted in his office while faces of Nicaraguan children popped in and out of his computer's screen saver. He'd grown up on a farm in north-central Iowa, in a small town called St. Ansgar three miles south of the Minnesota border. They'd lived simply and were "relatively poor," but Keith never knew they were poor. With his father he'd tended cattle and pigs, and grew corn and beans to sell at the cooperative elevator. With the few chickens they had, they ate eggs all week and on Sunday they ate the chicken. "It was a lot of eggs during the week and a lot of chicken on weekends," he said.

Driving the forty-five minutes it took to get to Branson later that day, the conversation lulled, fatigued from all the chatting in the office and over lunch. I sat in the back of their Acura and looked out the window to drink in the Ozarks. I played back in my mind stories I'd heard that morning relating to Keith and Karen's early life. They'd known one another since the sixth grade, two of twenty-seven members of the high school graduating class of 1961. At first they couldn't stand each other. By the time they were seniors they knew they'd be one another's life's mate. They'd attended college in Iowa, she at Iowa State, he at State University of Iowa, and married after the first year. Then Karen dropped out to raise the family. Keith had played first trombone in the school band and was majoring in music. To pay bills during college he worked at Kinney Shoes where he earned commission: two percent for shoes; five percent on socks and stockings; ten percent on arch supports. "I was leading the state and the chain on arch support sales," he'd said. "That helped me decide to go into business." He switched majors from music to business and was two and a half years away from graduating when he made the decision to drop out altogether and follow his business instincts. He worked his hardest at Kinney Shoes.

The day came when a man in a suit walked into the store and Keith sold him a pair of leather shoes, tennis shoes, socks, and, of course, arch supports. It turned out the man was district manager of Osco Drug. He returned the next day to offer Keith a job overseeing the purchasing of cookies and candies. At Osco Keith was putting in eighty-hour weeks and earned about ninety-five dollars a week. "It got tiresome," he'd said. The young family was only getting bigger and the financial demands more exacting.

He applied for a sales job at The Sather Cookie Company, which took him to Round Lake, Minnesota. He immediately won the trust and fatherly watch care of company owner Kenneth Sather. From Sather he learned what a business degree might never have taught him: "He kept encouraging me and gave me self-confidence and self-respect," Keith said. "I was a real back-country kid." Through bulldog tenacity, hard work, a willingness to go boldly where Sather himself wouldn't dare, within five years Keith had been instrumental in bringing net sales from three million to forty million dollars. "I told Kenneth I'd like to call on Kmart, and he said Kmart wouldn't be interested. I said, 'Probably not. But I'd like to try.'" A few years later Kmart gave Sathers twenty million dollars a year in business.

He spent nine years with Sathers "putting in the hours and not standing around talking," as Keith put it. He helped bring the company to a place where, eventually, they sold-out sweetly to Nabisco. Knowing now what he could do, Keith hankered for the rewards of owning and running his own business.

Fast forward through the purchase and sale of two bowling centers, one in Minnesota (1978) and the second in Springfield, Missouri (1982), both sold for considerably more than what he'd paid. Fast forward through a bold but alas unsuccessful run for the U.S. Congress in 1988 under the slogan "Putting People First." (Bill Clinton hired the same media group in his bid for the presidency, and they recycled the motto.) In 1990 he bought his first hotel, a Days Inn with 197 units, and went on to build the family hotel business from that base.

"Throughout this period I was very active with Habitat for Humanity," Keith had said. During the late seventies in Minnesota, he taught a junior high Sunday school class at a Presbyterian church and was always rooting around for books to share with the young people. He came across *Love in the Mortar Joints: The Story of Habitat for Humanity*, by Millard Fuller. At the time he and Karen were sensing a desire, as he put it, "to do more for Jesus." They became so enthralled with the premise of the book, that a month after they'd moved to Springfield, he and Karen drove to Americus, Georgia, to meet the author face to face. The book (and Habitat) asserts the idea of working to build decent affordable homes in partnership and side by side with the people who would inhabit them. In Springfield in the early eighties, he began working as a volunteer for Habitat. "I spoke in probably a hundred churches helping get Habitat started there locally." He served two terms as a board member, fundraising and working with Jimmy Carter and Tony Campolo and others, and another six years on committees. He oversaw the committee commissioned to hire an administrative director of the Americus office, which essentially reorganized internal operations. "When you hang around people like Millard Fuller, Tony Campolo, and Jimmy Carter for a lot of years, that rubs off on you," he'd said. During those years his economic successes blossomed while his sense of responsibility to empower the poor, through his exposure to Habitat, grew more acute. In all, he worked twelve years as a board member with Habitat, and many more as a volunteer. These years informed what I call his "theology of wealth."

"You take what you need for your children and family. Then you provide for your employees. Then you reach out beyond that. If you've got what you need, why would you want a lot more? That doesn't mean you shouldn't make a lot more. It just means you have to share it.

"There are so many references in the New Testament about how difficult it is for a rich person to inherit the kingdom of God. People with money need to be concerned about that. Everybody should be concerned about it. There are so many biblical references to working with the poor and helping the poor that if you believe in God and believe in the Bible you have to believe that that's the way it is. It's not an option. Luke 12:20 says, to whom much is given much is expected.

"Karen and I always promised each other and God that if we became financially successful we'd find a way to give a lot back. That became true for us in the hotel business. When we had the bowling center in town I was working forty to fifty percent of my time for Habitat as a volunteer and we were making significant donations." Habitat went broke every summer, he'd said, and Millard

Fuller hit him up for loans (along with other board members). "Millard would call me and would say, 'How much money you got in the bank?' I'd ask Karen and she'd say, 'Almost a hundred thousand.' Millard would say, 'Good. I need ninety thousand of it.' So we'd write a check for ninety thousand to get them through the summer. He said he'd give it back in the fall. We did that for five or six summers in a row and we always got it back."

After twelve years on Habitat's board, which facilitated growth from a budget of four-hundred thousand dollars a year to twenty million, the hankering returned. Keith caught a vision to go out on his own and launch a new foundation to serve the poorest of the poor. "We wanted to do something that wouldn't get done if we didn't do it," he said. "So we looked around and eventually started what is now Rainbow Network in Nicaragua in 1995."

## 5
## A SINGING BIRD

Branson is another place I'd never visited, but I sensed we were getting close when I started seeing billboards for "Big Food Choices" and The Haygoods. "Branson had a population of 6,500 when we bought our first hotel," Keith said. "Now it has seven million tourists a year." The largest attraction is the Silver Dollar City amusement park—that, and the fact that more factory outlet stores exist here than in any other U.S. city. Glitzy shows in the town's thirty-five theaters "filled more seats than Broadway," Keith said. Branson is like a family-values mini-Las Vegas minus the casinos. Wayne Newton got a cold reception when he told "suggestive jokes." We passed a billboard for the Osmond Brothers who, evidently, were still kicking around, and another one for John Davidson (also still kicking) and Shepherd of the Hills Inspiration Tower. "Roy Clark brought Hee-Haw here," Keith said, referring to the ho-down hillbilly show of the 1960s. "The Lennon sisters live here, and Roy Rogers's son, and Larry Welk." That would be Lawrence Welk's son. "Country Tonight uses Star Search kids." I marveled at how little I knew about the Heartland.

Our first stop was the second largest hotel of the Jaspers three in Branson, the Howard Johnson, with 344 rooms and four buildings. Keith dashed about checking with this manager about one thing and undertaking for the housekeepers about another thing. Four Quality Assurance Excellence Award banners hung in the lobby next to the one boasting Property of the Year, Number One in the chain for 2000. Keith showed me the coffee shop, Harold's Grill, named for his father whose photo hung near the entrance. Next we drove to the Days Inn, mother of all Jaspers hotels, with seven buildings, 423 rooms, and Keith's Branson office. As we pulled into the parking lot, a Latino woman named Migulina approached. She was the manager of the maids, and that day was distressed about the lack of help. ("Estelita, she needs help with the laundry.

Everybody working in Howard Yohnson.") Keith left to attend the crisis, and Karen and I were left on our own.

A quiet, dignified woman with happy eyes, a Shirley Temple smile, and flaxen silvery hair, Karen Jaspers holds the reins of hotel and Rainbow finances. We ambled around, first to the Days Inn lobby, where she told me she supervised interior design, from the framed print over the fireplace mantle to the flowers in planters by the door. Karen Jaspers purchases all office supplies, candy for vending machines, furniture, beds and lamps for all the rooms, carpets and fabrics for all drapes and bedspreads. Until seven years ago, she alone handled the purchasing and bookkeeping for all hotels, which involved managing millions. ("It's easy to lose track of the money you spend," she said.) She has since hired four employees who, under her administration, attend the bookkeeping for the hotels as well as for Rainbow.

We chatted in Keith's office on the lower level, not quite the eclectic mix as the Springfield office, but telling just the same. To the left, behind the desk, not far from a lone bowling pin perched on a shelf, Karen pointed out a framed photo of exploding nebulae—"astronomy is another of his hobbies," she said. "He'll take his telescope to Colorado and stay up half the night looking at stars." She didn't go along when he took these trips; she didn't do well sleeping in the back of a Durango. Keith returned and filled in the details about the star gazing. "I like looking for things invisible to the naked eye. A group of globular clusters is the prettiest thing there is, millions and millions of shining stars. Mostly, it's galaxies, star clusters, and nebulae I see. Sometimes you can see the Milky Way. On a good night I can find maybe twenty or thirty other galaxies. It's a wonderful time to be quiet and relaxed and close to God and the marvel of nature that He created," he said.

"I think they already lost the toilet bolts I ordered," Karen interjected.

"We're a long way from the farm at St. Ansgar," said Keith.

We stopped briefly at the Red Roof Inn, the "baby hotel" Keith calls it (105 rooms), before heading back to Springfield. "Each hotel brand has its own following," he said. "A Red Roofer wouldn't be caught dead in a Howard Johnson." I never would have known.

It was when we were back in Springfield, when Keith showed me his little corner of heaven on earth, that I saw a Keith I had not known during the travels to Nicaragua.

❖ ❖

Keith, Karen, and I passed through a door over which hung a little yellow sign: Choo Choo Xing, meaning the Train Room, or better, Train House, since it's the size of a three-car garage and a separate entity from the main house. I'd entered the world of O-gage Lionel trains: Burlington Northerns, Baltimore and Ohios, Illinois Centrals, and Lehigh Valleys. "There's eight or nine miles of wiring under there," said Keith pointing to the Train Yard where lonely engines, freight cars, and commuter cabs waited their turn on the tracks. Karen waved a hand, indicating her contribution to this happy world. "Over here"—to our right—"I'm going to do a Rocky Mountain thing. Over here"—to our left—"will be an Ozark Mountain thing."

Karen Jaspers

"Things" Karen did, I learned, enabled Keith Jaspers to do the things he did. The Ozark Mountain thing, yet unfinished, included a miniature landscape with a windmill, a bi-level plane ("'cause he used to fly, you know"—*No, I didn't know that*"), a shiny red tractor, a yellow school bus, and randomly placed Jersey cows. In the time it took Karen to show me her creation, Keith—toggle in hand—had mobilized five trains and two trolleys, the latter coming and going from miniature fairgrounds on the northern perimeter of the Ozark Mountain thing. I stood spellbound by the rush of O-gages rounding the tracks. Then the Chessie System locked up and we lost a few cars over the side. Keith stopped all trains. "Sometimes they come off the track 'cause he runs them too fast," said Karen. Keith climbed atop a table on the Ozark side, stepping over tracks and contorting his back and neck at excruciating angles to reset little wheels onto little tracks. "Be careful, don't hurt yourself," I said. He paid me no mind. He was fixing trains. In no time the Chessies and Burlingtons and Illinois and Ohios were passing in and out of tunnels and blowing past each other here, on the Ozark side, and there, on the Rocky Mountain side.

Before escorting me to his back patio, he showed me his telescope, stored under the parked trains (the size of a small apple barrel), and pointed out the sign on the bathroom door: Do Not Flush Toilet While Train Is in Station. He pulled a string to make the train whistle blow, and we said good-bye to the world of Lionel trains. We three sat quietly on the patio chatting like old friends.

"Most Nicaraguans have never seen a successful Nicaraguan," Keith said. "That's why we boldly ask for huge sums of money from wealthy people. The money isn't for me, it's for them. Millard Fuller's mentor, Clarence Jordan once said, 'We all should become monumental beggars for Christ.' We ought to be embarrassed if we aren't." He turned his head. "Look there." A hummingbird flew by in search of nectar. "We get three or four dozen of them sometimes," he said.

Beyond the sloping backyard, near the tree line in a hollow down by the river, a Sycamore's tender leaves were coming into maturity, drinking nourishment from the soil and reaching skyward for the sun. "Christianity is a verb," he said. "It's about rolling up your sleeves and getting dirty and making a difference in somebody's life. I read somewhere that so many Christians try to figure out how to get to heaven when they ought to be thinking about how to bring heaven here to earth."

A formation of Canada geese flew overhead. "We get three species of finches here," he said. "Mockingbirds and scissor tail flycatchers too."

Keith Jaspers is an ordinary man. But he is open to God's movements and willing to take leaps of faith that challenge modern sensibilities. Keith will climb tables and crane his back in excruciating angles to fix toy trains. If that were his last act on earth he'd die a happy death doing it. He cranes his back to look at galaxies. He's a doer because he's first a seer.

"Birds always find the air wherever they fly," wrote Francis de Sales. "So wherever we go or wherever we are, we find God present," holding us and giving us air for flight. Sometimes a singing bird lights in a knobby tree at the cusp of a smoking mountain. It sees something we don't see.

G. K. Chesterton said that people living in small medieval towns like Assisi, where St. Francis lived, knew only the life that fell within the bounds of those walls. These provincial towns "turned out names of Dante and Michael Angelo, Ariosto and Titian, Leonardo and Columbus." It is a "curious fact" he concludes, "that about three quarters of the greatest men who ever lived came out of these little towns."

    I drove home a happy person after my first visit to the Heartland. I learned there really is a place on this earth called Hillbilly Junction, right there on Route 60 heading east. I passed through it. I also learned there exists a place called Low Wassie a few hundred miles outside Winona. My country, where small towns breed ordinary people with miniature trains and telescopes to see things invisible to naked eyes, the prettiest things, millions and millions of shining stars. He sees galaxies in the eyes of Nicaraguans.

# Part III
## *Rhythms*

### 6
### GATHERING THE PIECES

The Rainbow Network board of directors had gathered that same spring for their biannual meeting at the Wingate Inn, the orphan Jaspers family hotel in St. Louis. Insofar as these good people strategized passionately on behalf of Nicaraguans, the implausibility of this picture bears noting. The Nicaraguan Revolution and subsequent post-civil war peace and self-determination had decisively repulsed U.S. interventionism. Yet the principal arm for lending a hand up (not a hand-out, as Keith likes to say it), has been the non-government organization, many of which are U.S. sponsored and funded by U.S. dollars, like Rainbow. When it comes to smoothing life's jagged edges and helping real people, ideologies defer to human spirit and hard work. This is what I saw brought to bear by decisions made and plans unfurled in the Rainbow board meeting I attended that spring.

Now might be the time to highlight how the country has faired since the peace agreement had ushered in the nation's first free elections in 1990. Coalition candidate for the newly formed National Opposition Union, Violeta Chamorro—widow of the martyred journalist Pedro Chamorro—decisively defeated Sandinista candidate Daniel Ortega. "After Somoza, the Revolution, and the ten-year civil war, there was too much misery, too much death, and too much economic desperation," said Rainbow director in Nicaragua, Peter Schaller. "The elections were about laying down arms." The figure of a woman gave the tenuous peace the comfort and consolation of a mother, Marcos had said. "She was a figure of reconciliation." Chamorro offered food and other benefits in exchange for the laying down of arms. Butts and barrels of hundreds of AK-47s jut from mounds of jagged concrete in a haunting memorial in downtown Managua called the Park of Peace.

For all the symbolism, the practical outworking of this new hope in Nicaragua proved onerous. Two more elections have since taken place (1996 and 2002) and the Sandinista party's Ortega "never came back" (to borrow from Peter). Liberal candidate (in U.S. terms, "conservative") Armando Alemán took office in 1996, promising tax incentives for the private sector while cutting spending on social programs. Under Alemán, "the upper echelon blossomed, but that has not trickled down to the masses," said Peter, the ninety percent of the 4.8 million who remain in poverty. Alemán "became like a little figure of Somoza," said Marcos. "He had a good life, you know—a lot of business under the table. He drove fancy cars." He is presently under house arrest for stealing his country's assets. The good news is, Alemán got there by means other than violent revolution. His successor and current president, Enrique Bolaños, has taken a resolute stand against corruption despite incredulity of his critics complaining he himself arose out of Alemán's shady administration.

For all its groping toward democracy, the Nicaraguan government's hands have been tied when it comes to elevating the conditions for those in greatest need. In 2000 Nicaragua surpassed Haiti as the poorest country in the Western hemisphere with a per capita GDP of $495. (It is now second to Haiti in this dubious distinction.) Three quarters of the population live on less than two dollars a day. The Ministry of Health runs hospitals and clinics, but they are understaffed and have no medicines. "When people are scheduled for an operation the hospital gives them a list materials to bring before they can be served, like gloves, gauze, and iodine," said Peter. Most rural communities have insufficient water systems. Many people must walk miles to springs or creeks for water. In one community the municipal government provided a truck with a tank to carry water, but there was no gas in the truck. "So much of government monies and efforts are tied up in administration and overhead. They are quite ineffective in reaching the poor who really need the services," said Peter. "NGOs are providing the only beacon of hope for this country."

❖ ❖

At its inception in 1995 Keith and Karen personally underwrote Rainbow's funding. Since then it has grown from a meager presence in five *comarcas* (rural communities) to eighty-eight, with more on the horizon. Their budget at the start was $80,000. In 2004, they budgeted nearly two million dollars.

For the first three years they did not solicit funds. Then they launched the scholarship program to help Nicaraguan young people complete high school. They availed to their church family the opportunity to participate in this program with gifts amounting to $22 a month. Keith said, "They jumped into that real quick." Keith gratefully received their support and then asked, "Could you do more?" But it wasn't until Hurricane Mitch devastated the region in 1998 that the big money came in. This galvanized Rainbow's present donor base which has remained robust.

Keith, staff, and board members plot strategically where greatest need is measured against surest feasibility. Once it has been determined where development can thrive, and after a series of meetings with the Nicaraguans in those communities, Rainbow waits for an official invitation to come and establish a "network." Its network sets up in a primary village, but with tentacles that reach several smaller communities within its environs. In each little town or neighborhood, they form committees for education, housing, economic development (microloans), and health care—their four targeted areas—and recruit local people as volunteers. Education committees search out people who can read and write and recruit them to help in the school program. Health care committees learn how to chlorinate water and manage parasite control. These people, in turn, teach neighbors and friends.

"For any program to work the people themselves must pitch in, whether as a teacher at the school; or providing labor in a housing project; or doing the

*Peter Schaller*

cooking and cleanup at a feeding center," Keith said. "They're going to build their own house. If they visit a doctor, they're going to pay the doctor something, even if only in beans and corn. They're going to pay back the loans. We talk at length so they understand the loans we make are only for entrepreneurial activity," said Keith. "We don't loan money for education or health care. We talk about the need to pay us back weekly or biweekly.

"We believe in hard work, dedicated work. We train volunteers to put in the hours and achieve specific goals. They're responsible for how they use their resources, whether it's cement for making a house, or books and pencils for the school, or sewing machines. When those goals are achieved, they take away a sense of satisfaction and accomplishment. We don't do these things for them to have a hobby."

At this writing, Rainbow operates six networks, each reaching as many as fifteen *comarcas*. Their efforts focus upon rural areas outside Managua, the out-of-the-way place "down at the end of the road," as one donor put it. Their two most recent networks have been established in the northern highlands outside of San Ramón outside the small city of Matagalpa.

For the most part, it works. Each village establishes a community "bank," a cooperative entity comprised of twenty or so families who've banded together to borrow money. Every member is responsible to see that his neighbor (often a brother or an aunt) pays back his or her part. "If one person pays off his loan while someone else is only half paid off, the first won't be able to get another loan until all of it is paid," said Karen. "Every person in the bank signs and agrees to pay on anyone within that bank who is delinquent."

"The Nicaraguan communities are accountable to themselves," said Keith. "These are projects for Nicaraguans, run by Nicaraguans." If a problem arises, the Rainbow staff person takes it to the local committee and leaves it to them to work it out with their neighbors. "Sometimes there may be a person who is burned out or unhappy and doesn't want to participate," he said. "This is God's work and the resources we use are God's resources. It doesn't benefit anybody if we put a worker in the field who can not carry out his mandate. You owe it to the people, you owe it go God, and you owe it to that person to change that face. That person will do better at a different kind of work. When people are not successful at one type of work, it doesn't mean they're bad. It simply means that for whatever reason they either are not qualified or not motivated to do this particular work in this particular location at this particular time. By working together with our staff in these conflicts, the committees and volunteers often come back with a motivated hard-working answer, rededicated to the work on a higher level.

"Rainbow Network may have had the dream and the vision, but the people in Nicaragua have got to want it, they've got to work it, they've got to do it," he said. "And they do."

"It is also important to know that Rainbow would not be what it is were it not for the hard work and ideas of many dedicated and generous people, hundreds of dedicated donors, dedicated churches, communities in Nicaragua themselves, and a dedicated board. Without those committees and that enthusiasm there would be no Rainbow Network."

Which brings me back to the board meeting in St. Louis and strange pinings that again came over me.

## 7
## WHAT IT TAKES TO BUILD A VILLAGE

The reader at this point might ask, why the digression narrating what, in my mind anyway, could serve as the working definition of boring: a "board meeting"—any board meeting. Gathered in a room around tables with bottled water, talking heads meet and make resolutions you'd think they thought kept the earth in its orbit. At this meeting, I was particularly at sea, knowing only a few, and fighting back an aversion to talking heads in small rooms behind closed doors. I'm a field journalist. I need air.

Therein lies the surprise and so the digression. I invite the reader to this meeting to hear voices of people—"board members"—so you can hear what I heard and see what I saw. These were not talking heads. They were ordinary people who gave up time and money to be here and discuss how best to help Nicaraguans. Their decisions, in fact, would keep the world of the lives they touched intact and in orbit.

I took a seat next to a man named Tom, a lawyer from Springfield. Tom pulled out my chair, greeting me, and said, "I'm Tom. Tell me about yourself and don't leave anything out." On my other side a familiar face, my friend Tim, who'd taken a jog in the rain that morning before joining the meeting. Next to Tim sat Rocky, a pharmacist, Robert Ulrich look-alike, and board chairman. Keith and Karen, respectively, sat next to Rocky. During the introductions Karen said, "I'm Karen Jaspers. That's all I have to report." Around the corner was a septuagenarian couple in jean jackets, Mel and Barbara. A purple-blazored Pat sat next to them, and by Pat sat Romona, laptop perched on her knees to record the minutes. Mark was next, a friendly faced fellow with a Gary Shandling look about him. Next to him were Al and Charlene, coexecutives of the Tin Roof Foundation, another NGO in Nicaragua. Up the other side of the conference table was Rainbow employee Alice and her husband Ron, the group photographer on the first trip. Then came Bob, an oncologist and kindhearted man who said he saluted the Nicaraguan Rainbow doctors for the work they accomplished under such challenging conditions. A tanned, sporty Betty completed the circle, whose husband is a lifetime friend of Keith. She learned about Rainbow at their high school reunion in 1996. A Disciples of Christ pastor named Roger would soon make an appearance, but he wasn't there when the time came to begin devotions, led by Mel.

"If I were to take the Christian life seriously, what would it look like? How do I know when I have arrived?" He used the Beatitudes as the point of reference. "There's only one thing we have that no one can take from us and that's our spirit," Mel said. "When we turn that spirit over to God and take on God's spirit, we become poverty-stricken in spirit. If we think like God we begin to mourn for the world. If we are meek before God, we begin to hunger and thirst for the right thing.

"How do we know when it's morning and the darkness is over? When we see olives growing on the olive trees," he said. "Blessed are the peacemakers. To make peace we have to be at peace—*shalom*—with ourselves, with God, and with our neighbor." Mel said, "The Christian life leads us to places we could not imagine going." Then he prayed, "Lord, keep us poor in spirit."

Shortly thereafter Roger appeared, self-defined "parish pastor in Springfield, Missouri." He presented Keith with a $40,000 check. Roger was in charge of raising $250,000 to build 200 houses in the northern mountain region of San Ramón. Keith said, "Thanks for the 40K, Roger, but what we really need is a quarter of a million."

Water bottles and pop cans neatly fixed on paper coasters, notebooks, and jars of peanuts at the ready, the meeting began with Karen's financial report, the details of which I will not delineate since these discussions make my eyes glaze over. I heard her say "year to date donations . . . [something] [something] . . . $248,000." She made more than one reference to the "dollar checking account and the 'cord' checking account" (*cordobas* are the Nicaraguan currency). I heard her say, "Our office is more Rainbow than Jaspers Hotels now" and how a fellow on our trip had given $50,000 as soon as he got home. She said something about "a cash flow deficit" at one point, adding that donations had picked up, and I was quite impressed by her self-possession. She had referred to "Nagarote," as if it had been her home town, though she's been to Nicaragua only once. At some point Keith said, "We gotta get more twenty-five, thirty—fifty thousand dollar hits."

Mark stepped up with his report which, evidently, was similarly related to finances, noted in a similar glossing over of my eyes. He said general donations were up thirty percent from last year, "bucking the trend in the decrease in giving for nonprofits." He specifically noted the generosity of foundations, which is when Tim chimed in: "You can't count on foundations to give year after year. A non-profit is more stable with a broader network of support. The best strategy"—Tim is quite thorough when it comes to strategies—"is to have multiple income streams." I thought, *If that doesn't sound like a lawyer. . . .* Tim added, "It's much easier to keep a donor you've got than to go out and get another one," and that made perfect sense to me. The same is true for magazine subscribers, and magazine subscribers are something I know a little about.

A discussion ensued about the cost of a house in their housing projects: $1,300 for a six-by-eight-meter cement block home with steel structures, the kind of home they want to build in San Ramón with the $250,000 Roger is raising. "I'm eating this elephant in thousand-dollar increments," Roger said.

Betty said Rainbow thanks their donors well. Mel said it was high time somebody wrote a book about Nicaragua and how their lives were changing because of this work. Keith laughed and explained that's why I'd come: to watch how ordinary people in one station of life change lives of other ordinary people in another station. He said my being there was a miracle.

The topic of miracles moved the discussion to the needs in San Ramón. In that mountain region poverty reaches appalling levels. Rainbow had recently established fifth and sixth networks there. "Dirt in San Ramón is softer than dirt in Ciudad Sandino," Keith said, meaning that people with dirt floors in Ciudad Sandino are better off than people with dirt floors in San Ramón. "We marvel at someone who can have a clean dirt floor."

Thus began the protracted discussion about prefabricated housing construction, its pluses and minuses, and that's when strange longings came over me.

The catalyst for debate had been the distance, bad roads, desperate conditions, and soggy weather in the mountains. Wouldn't it be more expedient to put up prefabricated concrete homes quickly, let the people move in, and then have them "work it off" (so to speak) in community service of other types?

"There's a lot involved in development. We don't just hand it to them," Keith said. "Families need to build their houses if it takes them five or six months. If we go in and build it for them, it's just another government project."

"Slab concrete prestress wall? I don't see that being able to happen up there," said Roger.

"You can stay ahead of the drizzle with tarps," said Al.

Pat interjected, "Doesn't the time it takes to build these homes help create a community?"

Tim responded, "We send workers down for a week. Don't you feel community in a week?"

Al and Charlene chimed in together, "We are not impressed with prefab concrete houses."

"How they would deliver a prefab wall to a place up there is beyond me," said Roger.

Someone answered (I didn't catch who): "It's in pieces. It's not the complete wall."

Tim said, "The issue for me is, what will stand up in a hurricane?"

"Does a duplex put families too close together? That would save on a wall," said Mel.

Keith said, "I don't like it. It puts people too close together. I can see lots of problems down the road. We can get the cost down by eliminating the kitchen, get it down to twenty-nine square meters."

"I'd rather try and raise more money than build smaller houses," said Roger.

Here is where the longings that had been chasing me caught up to me. When you're a writer, you're never inside the story. You're outside the story. You're listening for dialogue and looking for twitches or nervous habits. You do not vest yourself in which side prevails. It is nothing to you whether they lug up the mountains wall chunks or concrete block or brick. Or whether they decide to set up a brick-making factory first, then build brick houses—an option also considered in that discussion. You are not part of the conversation, which means you are not part of the story.

The feeling that had haunted me, contrary to my vocation, was a desire to enter the story. I listened to the passion in these voices; the coherence as one comment played off the preceding one, and sometimes the incoherence as they didn't; the willingness to disagree; and the excruciating meticulousness with which they assessed the surest way to build good houses for the people of San Ramón, and I thought, *There are notes to take and quotes to get and I must keep my distance in order to take and get them. You are a visitor listening in on someone else's conversation. You are not one of them. Your pen and notebook are the place you call home.*

Charlene said, "We're definitely not impressed with prefab houses. Keith, would it make more sense to hire more overseers at each project?" I wanted to say, *Well, does it? I really want to know.*

"I'm leaning toward the brick and mortar solution," said Keith.

"It's not like the rain forest up there. It doesn't rain constantly," said Charlene.

Tim added, "Another point would be the ease of repair. If you build your home brick by brick you're going to know how to repair it if it breaks."

"As far as laying block on a rainy day, that's not unheard of even in the U.S.," said Keith. "You just put up a tarp and work under it."

"Most creativities are pure logic," said Mel.

Tim possessed nervous energy and pulled out his chair to stand.

"We'll probably go with a thirty-year mortgage," said Keith. "You're dealing with a currency that's being devalued all the time. The value of the cord they're paying us back with is a fraction of the cost of what we paid for it in dollars."

"Concrete seems to be a stable factor in pricing through the years," said Mel, who then corrected himself—"Cement, actually."

Someone said, "Thirty years in Matagalpa, you can't predict what kind of social upheaval might take place."

"If we had those loans thirty years ago," added Roger, "we would have faced an invasion, a revolution, a civil war, an earthquake, and a hurricane."

Charlene said, "The hope is that children receiving education will come up with a solution for how to make this work."

❖ ❖

Are journalists who tell these stories beyond the reach of miracles? Are we beyond the story? I was on the outside looking in. I wondered in this meeting if there might be a way in, even for a reporter. I sensed it did not require a vow as if, say, I'd wanted to join the Franciscan Order of the Poor Clares. It was the sort of vow that said, there is nothing the world holds on me; it has me only by the fringe of my garment. These were the same yearnings I'd sensed along mountain roads; that had stirred hearing Marcos speak memories of his youth; that had awakened in me watching birds fly upward on the Jaspers' patio. Here, in this conference room in the Wingate Inn, I began to understand the work of this NGO as the rhythm of a poem. The troubadour was singing his song. He was inviting others to join in. I saw only ordinary people in that room, an old man in a jean jacket, a woman in a blazer, a doctor saluting Nicaraguans, a lawyer who jogs in the rain. Keith said, "Jesus performed miracles because he was the Son of God. We are the sons and daughters of the same God," he said. "Miracles still happen. Anybody can be a part of them, ordinary people." He was not meaning the hem-touching kind that Jesus manifested in spectacular moments. He meant the ordinary kind: a doctor salutes Nicaraguans and helps them learn to heal; a teacher goes to the countryside to drill a well; a lawyer funds business loans that start up sewing co-ops and chicken farms. Keith had said even my presence at that meeting was a kind of miracle.

"Violence will disappear from your land; the desolation and destruction of war will end," the prophet says. "Salvation will surround you like city walls, and praise will be on the lips of all who enter there" (Isa. 60:18). One might call it a revolution signaling that the darkness is over and morning has come. Mel said, "The Christian life leads us to places we could not imagine going"—and here I was, wanting a way in to the spirit of a board meeting! *I feel like I'm taking crazy pills!* Blessed are the poor who long for God's heart, Mel had said. It is like a poem, lovely and true and revolutionary, so human in its simplicity, I'd give away my pen to hear it, to sing it.

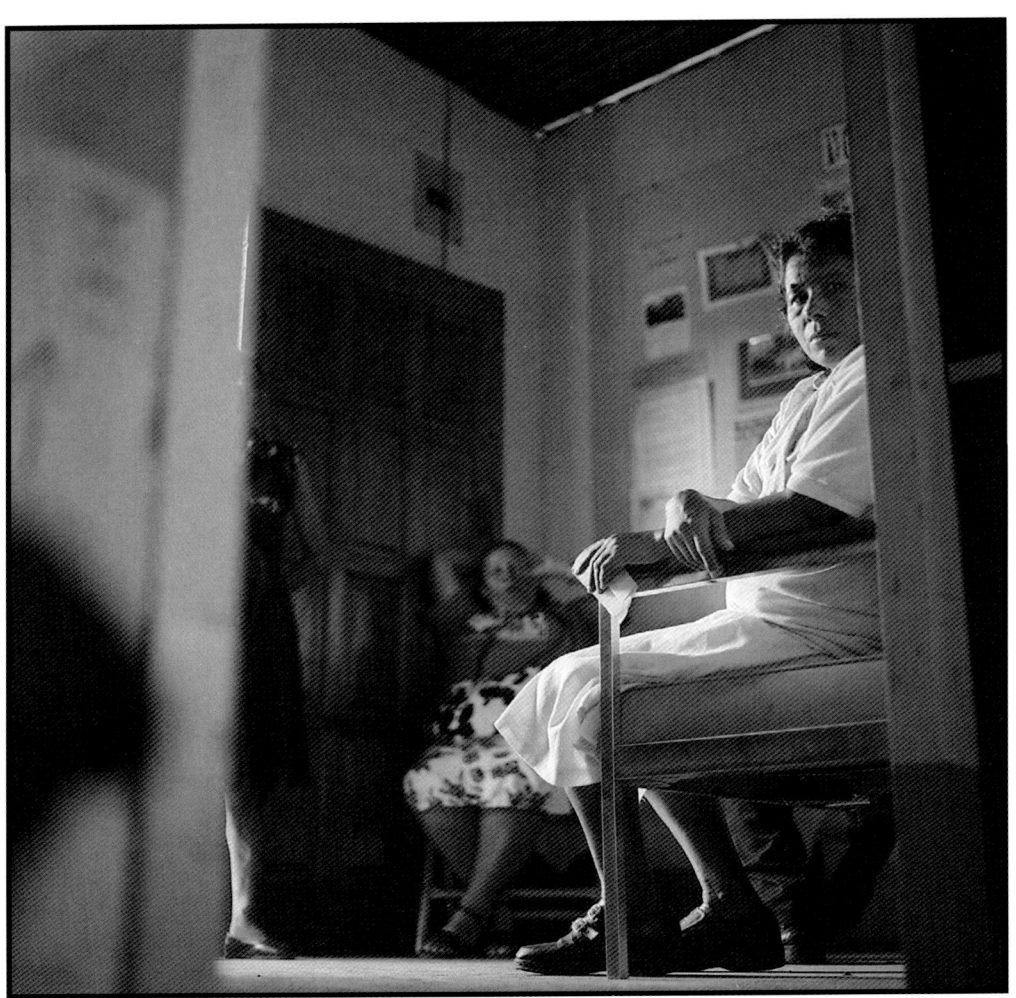

# The Second Journey

*You are singing Your song
in the hearts of the poor.*

—James K. Baxter

# Part IV
## *The Song*

I'd asked myself at the Rainbow board meeting, *Are journalists who tell these stories beyond the reach of the story?* I found the answer on my second trip to Nicaragua. I arrived in Managua on July 19, 2003, the day marking the twenty-fourth anniversary of "the triumph of the Revolution," as Marcos had called it. I'd returned on my own, my son Jon as my traveling companion, to meet one-on-one with the Nicaraguan people whom I'd seen only in glimpses on the previous trip. Then, they'd been anonymous—blurred faces in crowds that had gathered to welcome Mister Keith. This time, Jon and I sat in their homes where beans cooked over fires, and we sat under trees with pigs and chickens at our feet. We saw mothers and fathers touching their children, old men with machetes, little girls watching from afar with curiosity. And this time, when the people spoke, we heard in their words the sound of singing.

Our visits followed a concentric circle, starting in Rainbow's networks closest to Managua: Ciudad Sandino and El Crucero. Then we moved farther west to their network in Nagarote, then farther still—north to the mountains and Rainbow's newest network in San Ramón, where Marcos still trembles when he remembers.

# 8
## CIUDAD SANDINO

*Ciudad Sandino* is named for the revolutionary hero Augusto César Sandino, for whom the Sandinistas were named. It is a barrio on the outer edges of Managua and the locus of Rainbow's earliest efforts in 1995. Their operation's headquarters remain here, overseen by Peter Schaller, an American married to a Nicaraguan, and who is director in Nicaragua of the Rainbow Network. It's also where famed baseball star Roberto Clemente had been headed when he died in a plane crash bringing aid to the Nicaraguan people after the earthquake of 1972.

## "I Am Always Praying for Peace"

### Aleyda Hernandez

*Trinidad Central was once terrorized by Somoza's National Guard. During one of Rainbow's first visits here, Keith had been talking with the community about how Rainbow could partner with them to develop an education program. In the heat and cramped environment, he was growing fatigued and kept checking his watch. Finally, the session was winding down when a "little woman" raised her hand. "Children are fainting in the school because they are hungry," she said. Keith settled in for a long talk with her, resulting in Rainbow's setting up a feeding center along with the educational program.*

*That "little woman" is Aleyda Hernandez, thirty-five, who teaches in that same program. A petite woman, as an advocate for the community she looms large in the eyes of her neighbors.*

❖ ❖

I grew up in a time when National Guardsmen knocked on doors, pulling villagers from their homes, accusing them of sympathizing with the Sandinista rebels. I witnessed neighbors being killed and hands of others being cut off with machetes. In those years of war, we had many guests in the house. We were helping feed them and hide them because some men were behind them trying to kill them. The most terrible thing was when we would see people lying dead. I saw four or five people dead on the ground. The truth is, I don't like to talk about it because I always feel sad. It was a hard time to be living. I don't want to live it again. I'm sorry I cannot speak. The words don't come easily.

Aleyda Hernandez

There is a person here who is very poor. He is not my friend. He is not my relative. But I want to help him in the name of God. I feel very happy when people like Mister Keith come and bring us support. That is why I want to help him and help my community. That is why I am always praying for peace.

❖ ❖

*I am confident that I will see the LORD's goodness*
*while I am here in the land of the living.*
*Wait patiently for the LORD.*
*Be brave and courageous.*
*Yes, wait patiently for the LORD.*

—PSALM 27:13–14

# "The Food Is Ready Here"

## Yamilét Concepción Lopez

*Sitting at school desks on a concrete porch, we chat with Yamilét Concepción Lopez, thirty. Her home was also a meeting place for neighbors and visitors who wanted something to eat. She calls it "fast food," a small business she launched through Rainbow's microloan program. Hens and chicks amble at our feet while thunder rolls somewhere beyond. Her two little girls, ages three and four, hover nearby.*

I have a small business, selling fast food, like enchiladas. I make them and sell them to the community from my house. From six o'clock on in the evening they know the food is ready here. They ask me, "What are you going to make today?" and they tell me what they want. My specialty is enchiladas and tortillas. From the microloan, four months ago, I used the money to buy a freezer. But it was not working because the electricity is not stable. We were unable to pay back the loan, so I gave the freezer back. I am doing my fast-food business, and we also rent the land. My husband is a farmer. We have a big garden with corn, watermelon, and tomatoes. So the loan is all paid off. We are waiting for another opportunity for a loan. I am organizing the chicken raising project. White ones, like that one [pointing to our feet].

Right now my husband has a fracture in his leg. A tree fell over and broke his leg. He's been like that for four months. At four o'clock in the morning he was working out in the field, trying to get firewood and he had the accident. He was at my mother's house. My mother and brother were with him and took him to the hospital. The doctors from Rainbow have been a benefit to him. Every Friday the doctor comes here.

One of the things I pray about very hard is that I would like my husband to be healed. He's a big support for me. Sometimes my business is slow. I have no fast-food customers coming tonight.

❖ ❖

*He also turns deserts into pools of water,*

*the dry land into flowing springs.*

—PSALM 107:35

Yamilét Concepción Lopez

# "I Think Positively Always"

## David Ubeda

*David Ubeda, thirty-five, lost his childhood to Nicaragua's civil war. He was twelve when he joined the Sandinista guerrilla army. Until he was twenty-three, he stalked the mountains, carrying a six-shell carbine on his back. In 1996 his community selected him to put his name in the lottery for Rainbow's first housing project. Once he had been selected, he worked two days a week, building his home, the very first house erected by the Rainbow Network in Nicaragua. Married, with four children (eleven, nine, seven, and twenty months), the sign over David Ubeda's portal reads:* Casa #1, Familia Ubeda y Gamez. Dios lo es todo. *(God is everything.)*

About seven years ago we were taking care of a piece of land six kilometers from here. We lived in a house of tin walls half this size. The door was a curtain with two slats of wood. The community saw we were in need. Rainbow bought this land and we began to build our home.

When the civil war between Nicaraguans began, I was a boy and we were very poor and living in the mountains in the northern part of the country. They [the Contras] were killing people. At the age of twelve, when I was in sixth grade, I was strong enough to hold a backpack, so I was recruited. I used to be in school for six months. Then for the other six months I was mobilized to be in the mountains, fighting the Contras. In school we were told we had to do this because this was the order that came from higher up. The teacher told us those who didn't go would be

David Ubeda

out of school. The teacher had more authority than the parents. That was the way it was. I began doing that in 1981.

When you are a boy and get to go with your group, you say, "Let's go," and that's it. "*Vámonos*." I was carrying a gun and shooting a BZ rifle [a carbine] with six bullets. We did what we had to do. Then we come back.

When I was in school, the only thing I had in mind was just to go to school. My parents used to tell me, "You've got to go to school. You've got to be prepared." But when I was fourteen, I made up my mind to take the gun and fight the Contras all the time, instead of being six months in school and six months in the war. I was not afraid. I was ready to die. I felt no conviction about carrying a gun and shooting. That is what I wanted: to carry a gun. You do have the feeling that you don't want to shoot anybody. But given the war situation, if I don't kill, I'm going to get killed, although in your heart you feel you're not going to kill anybody. It's a hard situation.

For twelve years I was in the army. Daily I promised the Lord that if I leave the army alive when the war is over, I would serve him. Then peace talks began in the late 1980s and I began to think about trying to serve the Lord. It was a conversion coming out of my own heart.

In 1993, when Violeta [Chamorro] was in power, I left the army. Even then the military wanted to send me out to serve in a different way. But I didn't want to be in the army anymore. I joined voluntarily and I left voluntarily. There had been so much dying. I had made a promise to the Lord. I put the army aside and followed the Lord. I belong to the Church of God here in my village.

I am the first beneficiary of the first Rainbow housing project on the national level. Mine is the first house that was built, casa number one. I am jobless now and can't work because I've been ill as a consequence of those twelve years I was in the army. I got a lung disease. The church helps me, and my wife goes to work for three days, and I am here taking care of my children. We are in the first phase of talks with Rainbow about a loan to raise chickens.

I don't want my children to go through what I've been through. I'd like to teach them the righteous way. I've got to think positively always. According to the word of God, faith is a certainty of something we are unable to see.

❖ ❖

*I have stilled and quieted myself,*
*just as a small child is quiet. . . .*
*Yes, like a small child is my soul within me.*
*. . . put your hope in the Lord—*
*now and always.*
—Psalm 131:2–3

# "I See the Hand Trying to Reach Me"

Maritza Herrera Solarzano

*Up until last year, Maritza, twenty-nine, thought she did not exist, or in any case considered herself more like an animal than a person. As an infant she was abandoned by her mother and left on the street. She was rescued by an old man, who raised her, but she never had a birth certificate, which, in her mind, invalidated her life. She has born six children to a man who is not her husband (unable to marry without a birth certificate, in her thinking), and lives on a dusty patch of ground in a hovel made of a random assemblage of wood slats and tin. Her husband can't work because of an injury incurred a year ago. She is boiling beans over an open fire, which on a good day her children will eat twice.*

*To make matters worse, she struggled through each pregnancy with unmanaged blood sugar fluctuations from diabetes, causing her to exhibit behavior likened to paranoia. For years, she'd received little medical attention and had been dismissed without treatment, with the conclusion that her case was hopeless. Two years ago, Rainbow established a presence in her village, and she came under the care of their doctor. She has received medication to stabilize her sugar level and her children have been treated for malnutrition. Crowning this, her adopted father secured her a birth certificate this past year. She now believes she exists.*

We are very poor. If we had been left on our own it would not be possible to live. About a year ago my husband was working as a day laborer and something got into his eye. He can't see with that eye. It's not good for him to be in the sun. He is experiencing

*Maritza Herrera Solarzano*

pain in that eye during the night when he's been in the sun all day.

Sometimes we are able to provide two meals a day for our children. Some days just one. Right now I am boiling beans. We ate one time today in the morning. We will eat again in the evening. Just beans, no tortillas. We eat them boiled like soup. Sometimes we eat nothing during the day because we depend upon the land. When we are unable to feed our children, I go with my father-in-law into the field and hunt for armadillos. I feel bad about killing the armadillo. I do it with a knife. But given the necessity, I have to do it. I also work in the field. When it is harvest time, I harvest corn.

I belong to the Catholic church. All the people who go to the church are poor like I am. The priest is not here all the time because he comes from far away. When the person is married, then the person takes the sacrament. But we are not married, and we are not allowed to take the sacrament. I was never baptized because I never had a father or a mother. My parents abandoned me when I was a couple of days old. I felt as if I was like an animal, not a person, because I did not have a birth certificate. There was an old man who adopted me as his daughter. He gave me his last name, but I wasn't baptized. I felt as though I didn't exist. I am nothing. Nobody is watching me.

I have diabetes. Sometimes it goes so high, and sometimes it goes so low. It is a problem. I went to a doctor here who told me there is nothing he could do. "You are in danger," he said. "You are at risk." My baby boy was born with cephalic problems. Then the Rainbow doctor came to our community and told me I'm going to be under control. "We'll be taking care of you and your children," he said. They took control of my sugar and diabetes. My baby is doing okay now. I don't want to have any more children because the burden gets heavy. We are looking for the right time to be operated on [for sterilization] when the sugar is not giving me problems. Of course, I'm afraid I'll get pregnant before the operation. Seven kids? That's too hard.

We hope to get married someday. I would like to be baptized because we both as a couple would like our children to be raised like other children. When I am baptized and married, I will be able to take the sacrament. From the spiritual point of view, we will have life.

Sometimes when I feel I am nothing and nobody is watching me, then I see the hand trying to reach me. I see there is hope. The Rainbow doctor gave me hope that God sends someone to each of us to give us hope in life. One thing we like most as parents is not to see our children with tears in their eyes. God is the one who keeps us alive. I see the hand that is trying to reach me.

*I love the LORD . . . because he bends down and listens.*

*I will pray as long as I have breath! . . .*

*The LORD's loved ones are precious to him.*

—Psalm 116:1–2, 15

# 9
# EL CRUCERO

*El Crucero* is about thirty miles south of Managua. It rests high on a ridge leading south along the Pan-American Highway. Many wealthy Nicaraguans have built sprawling whitewashed homes on this ridgeline, lending it the name *Meseta de los Pueblos Blancos*—Plateau of White Towns. Amid private schools and coffee farms former President Alemán serves his time here under house arrest on one of his plantations. Beyond the whitewashed towns, shaded by cedars, along the ridge, with its jutting escarpment, lies another neighborhood. There homes are mud-thatched with outhouses and bamboo fences. Here live two of Nicaragua's noteworthy treasures—one still a child, the other a teen with dignity and self-possession beyond her years. Both carry dreams awakened by Rainbow: one holds dreams of a grown-up life in which fears give way to acts of kindness. The other carries the dreams of Nicaraguan women and the promise they possess.

# "I Felt I Needed to Give Thanks"

## Juana Santana

*The day we met under a tiled roof patio to talk, Juana Santana, ten, clutched her notebook. The year before, she'd received the notebook, colored pencils, and a doll as a Christmas gift from Rainbow. She took the initiative to travel the great distance to Ciudad Sandino for the purpose of thanking them for the gifts. She is the youngest of three, her older sisters, ages nineteen and twenty-two, being more like mothers. She stood poised and erect, hands clutched behind her back, a kitten playing at her feet. Now and then she pushed back hair from her face.*

My doll is very pretty. Her name is Ana because I like that name. I play with Ana. She is my little girl. I kiss her and hug her. She wears little skirts and blouses. Sometimes I change her clothes when she goes to parties. There are lots of people at the parties. They are dancing.

They also gave me colored pencils and notebooks. I draw pictures of houses and children and trees with the pencils. I draw red and yellow flowers. My favorite color is red. I use the notebook for geometry. [She shows me her notebook and reads what she has written.] "How can you classify the angles? The angles can be classified, if they measure less than ninety degrees, as acute. A right angle is ninety degrees and an obtuse angle is more than ninety degrees."

I went down to Ciudad Sandino with my uncle. I wanted to go

Juana Santana

because I was happy. I wanted to give thanks for the gifts. I don't remember who was there. I told them I was very grateful for the gifts. I felt I needed to give thanks to those people because they were giving me toys.

This Christmas I am hoping for another doll to be the friend to Ana. I will name him Juan, Ana's boyfriend. Juan will have black hair, a tall guy and handsome. He will be kind and in a nice mood. He will take care of me and help me. I do not have fears, only dreams.

❖ ❖

*When you send your Spirit, new life is born*
*to replenish all the living of the earth.*
—Psalm 104:30

# "Women Have Suffered"

## Ericka Fabiola Acuña

*Ericka Fabiola Acuña, seventeen, had already emerged as a leader in her community when Rainbow began their work there. Parents of children had recognized her gifts, both in academic accomplishment and in her way with children. When she was in her final year in high school, they asked her to assume the role of teaching the children, which she was happy to do. Rainbow quickly recognized her talents and standing in the community, and asked her to oversee their microloan program there. Later, with a loan she secured from the same program, she and her sister and mother started a sewing co-op, overseen by her mother. Before then, her mother worked as a maid in Managua while Ericka assumed the responsibilities of the household, caring for her five younger siblings. The work in the co-op has allowed her mother to stay home, earning more money per month than she did as a maid. In addition to Ericka's responsibilities in the community, she has used her income from the co-op to attend university on Saturdays, where she is studying to become a lawyer.*

I am attending the university in Managua to study law. It is a very interesting career and connected to all the things happening in the country. I go to class on Saturdays all year. I take two buses; one from here to the main road and then another bus to Managua. It takes five years to be a lawyer. I will graduate in four more years. I would like to defend the poor because I have been living in poverty and live among the poor. I would like also to defend women because they have suffered a lot.

I was chosen by the community to be the coordinator of the microloan program. The coordinator receives applications of people who want to borrow. I fill out the form with the people. I can help them do that. The decision about who gets the loans is made both by Rainbow and members of the community. The person must be a serious worker and punctual with the payments.

The money from the microloan enabled us to start this sewing program. The director of the Rainbow office in El Crucero told me I could gather people together so we could have a sewing cooperative here. Rainbow had the idea. Then there was a meeting with all the members of the community and they decided they wanted to bring it here and needed someone to oversee it. The boss is my mother. I am in charge of the finances. When items are sold, I get the money and distribute it, part to be invested in the work to buy material, and the other part to the workers. They are paid by the number of days and hours they work.

Before, most of the mothers were going out of the city to find a job, leaving their children alone. Today they can take better care of our children because they have a job here.

*Your throne is founded on two strong pillars—*
*righteousness and justice.*

—Psalm 89:14

Ericka Fabiola Acuña

# 10
# NAGAROTE

It is a big day when Jon and I visit Nagarote, a cattle town forty miles west of Managua. To get here, we'd driven dusty roads, passing ox-drawn carts—the kinds of back roads where Marcos would turn from the front seat to say, "Hold on, hold on." We pulled into a grassy field where, in the distance stood twenty-five brand-new concrete-block houses in two rows, facing each other, a Rainbow housing project. This is the day happy owners gather to claim their new dwellings amid songs, prayers, and balloons. I stand under a Tigalote tree, cicadas humming in the background, where little boys play games with stones and the mayor speaks into a scratchy microphone: "The Bible says by his deeds you will know him." Women in white dresses twirl and dance, ruffled collars off their shoulders and flowers in their hair. Someone sings, Ahh yaa yaa yaa. Then a little boy reads a poem. His name is Carlos Antonio Martinez Reál. He is happy this day. He has written the poem for Mister Keith.

> My mother was singing a song of happiness to me.
> But a gray evening came to me. My mother was saying good-bye.
> She was giving me kisses saying, "Do not cry, my son.
> I will not leave you alone."
> It was a bitter evening, full of pain.
> Everything was going dark. My mother was not returning to me.
> The hands I felt, when my mother said good-bye,
> were taking with them my mother's life.
> I asked God to comfort me, to take my mother inside heaven,
> I asked him to help me in this pain.
> My mother, who is at the side of God,
> knows more than anyone what I feel today in my heart.

# "I Pretend I Am a Goalie"

## Carlos Antonio Martinez Reál

*Carlos Antonio Martinez Reál, ten, lost his mother a year earlier. He is in fifth grade, studying Spanish and multiplication tables. He, his younger brother (seven), and older sister (twelve) live with his grandparents, the parents of his mother. He does not know his father.*

Mister Keith came once to our community, and I was chosen to welcome him. Then we became friends. He was giving me help with school supplies. That's why I write poems to him. I feel like he is sending my mother's love from heaven.

When my mother died words came out of my thoughts and I was able to write those words in a notebook. I am able to write as fast as the words come to my mind. When I am sad the words come up from my mind. Right now I am not sad. Maybe next time you come back I will have a poem for you.

My grandfather is a farmer. He grows corn and squash. My favorite thing to eat is rice with real beef. When my grandpa works and sells firewood, we get some money. Then we buy the rice and beef. I have roosters and hens. I don't play with them because right now they have a disease, and if I hug them they die. When they don't have diseases I like to hug them. I don't know how long they will have this disease. My grandpa, he's the one that knows.

I take prayers to my mother, like the Lord's Prayer. I don't hear my mother speak to me. My mother has talked to my

*Carlos Antonio Martinez Reál*

grandmother and aunt. She is saying to take care of my older sister because there are boys in the neighborhood trying to pick on her. I am taking care of my sister, but she doesn't listen to me. It's hard to take care of my sister when she doesn't listen to me.

I like soccer but I don't play because I don't have a ball. I pretend there is a world where I am the person who is a goalie. It is a nice thing to have dreams of being a goalie.

*Can my dust praise you from the grave? . . .*
*Help me, O LORD. . . .*
*You have taken away my clothes of mourning*
*and clothed me with joy.*
—PSALM 30:9–11

# "The Struggle Donated Thousands and Thousands of Lives"

Alexis Castillo

*Alexis Castillo, thirty-seven, serves as Rainbow's committee coordinator in that new neighborhood. He also belongs to a sewing co-op making aprons, shirts, shorts, and towels to sell in the marketplace. He is married with two children, ages five and seven. His son Derling Moises, is wheelchair bound, having suffered meningitis as a baby. The fever crippled him. Rainbow provided the wheelchair, medical attention, milk, and medicine. His son "smiles like any other kid," Alexis says. He is also nearly blind, but is "very smart and listens to people. If you come to our home and he hears your voice, he would know immediately that you're not from that house." Alexis, like most Nicaraguan males his age, fought in the Sandinista army. Unlike many, however, he was sympathetic to the ideologies of the party and fought for the principals espoused by the Sandinistas. He has since understood its weaknesses, but remains committed to the ideal of equality among the people.*

I was the leader of the Sandinista party and would follow the ideology of the Sandinistas. I fought as a Sandinista.

In Cuba I was taught how to work with dogs along the borders. I was inspired by Castro in the struggle. I used to see him as a supporter of the Sandinista revolution and still see him that way. I admire him up to a certain point. A true politician should give space to democracy. I love the Cuban people. But I pity them because Castro does not let his people choose what they want. I don't like Castro in a personal way, but I like his stand against injustices in the world.

I got wounded in the war. I've got a piece of shrapnel in my thigh. The war changed me. When you are in the mountains you are able to see the suffering of the people. That's why I made a decision to fight for what we had won through the revolution. The counter-revolutionaries were being backed by the most powerful country in the world, the United States. The revolutionary struggle had donated thousands and thousands of lives, and overnight, the most powerful country wanted to take that from us.

I try to get people involved in different projects with the Rainbow Network so we can learn how to work together as a community. If there is a disagreement, I call the people together to find some middle ground, a point where we can come together in agreement. It is not an easy job. I also have to be a peacemaker. The war taught me how to love and to struggle for the poor, the most humble people. Rainbow taught me how to work with love in my heart. I have learned how to be a peaceful person.

*[I] thank you, O God!*
*When the earth quakes and its people live in turmoil,*
*[You are] the one who keeps its foundations firm.*
*—Psalm 75:1, 3*

Alexis Castillo

## *"Have Faith in God to Make Dreams Come True"*

Mercedes Rojas Rios

*Marcos and I sit on the front step of casa #25, the last house at the end of the row in the new housing project. It belongs to Mercedes Rojas Rios, who had just learned that house would be her new home. Marcos and I needed a break, having spent the morning interviewing more people than I could count, Marcos translating every word. We are tired, hot, and hungry. He eats his rice and beans; I eat my granola bar. Mercedes waits just beyond, allowing us the use of her front step. Before we resume our interviewing, I say to Marcos, "You ready?" He says, "I am always ready. I am a warrior—a guerrilla." I say, "If you are a guerrilla, what does that make me?" He says, "I am a guerrilla and you are a gorilla." (Remember our mutual love of wordplay?)*

*Mercedes Rojas Rios, thirty, approaches and joins us on the front step. She is happy to share with us her new home, casa #25. Soon she would live there with her husband and two daughters, ages eight and eleven. The breeze cools our faces as we chat.*

I was asking God to have the benefit of having a home. I wanted to provide a home for my children. My husband used to work in agriculture but he got sick with kidney problems. Now he is jobless. I work as a maid. When people need my service they look for me and tell me to do laundry or ironing. It gives us just enough to maintain us. I need to earn a little more. Once I am settled in here I'll have to leave for Managua because in Managua people get paid better. I will come back home every weekend.

I pray to God to provide help for my husband. The doctor

Mercedes Rojas Rios

from Rainbow Network has given him some medicine. Now he's taking pills. He is getting better. If my husband finds a job I won't have to leave my home to work in Managua. I can take care of my daughters because they are growing up. Girls, once they are fourteen years old, are in danger. The older one is going into her first year in high school. I heard a story that a lady saw a naked man on the road to Nagarote. I'm afraid that somebody can rape my daughters on the way to school. The school is six kilometers from here.

We must ask God and be faithful. I used to think having a house for my family was like a dream, and I could never think like that. The way I got my home, through Rainbow Network, showed me that if we ask God with faith, God will provide what you need. That's what I believe. If you say a prayer without faith, God won't hear. Have faith in God to make dreams come true.

❖ ❖

*Replace the evil years with good.*
*Let [me] see your miracles again;*
*let [my] children see your glory at work.*
—PSALM 90:15–16

# "I Was the Tutor of My Children"

## Melanio Ocampo Figuora

*Melanio Ocampo Figuora was living with his father, mother, a brother, and two children (one of whom was his) when his application to receive and build a house with Rainbow was approved. The joy of receiving his new home was, however, bittersweet. He had recently learned that his wife, who was working in Costa Rica, would not be returning to live with him in the new house. Two of his three children are with her. He doesn't know when he'll see them again.*

*He had been asked to pray spontaneously earlier that day at the housing project dedication.*

I told my wife that I was going to have a new home and she said, "I'm glad to hear that." She told me that she didn't know whether she would be living with me in the home. That's when I came to understand she doesn't want to be with me anymore. We've been married for seven years. We have three kids. I used to have them with me but she took two of them away. I was the tutor of my children. She didn't have the right to take my children. I feel I've lost my children. My nine-year-old is still here, living with me.

I am a mason. But there are no job opportunities. I am also a farmer, and agricultural work provides money for us to get ahead. I hope to plant a garden when I move into this house. Just I and my son will be living here. I need to talk to Rainbow to see if someone can come take care of my son so I can leave and try to find work. My son is in first grade. I will be moving in two weeks. Of course I am excited about it.

I wasn't nervous about praying because I was an instrument of God. He was using me in that moment to say the prayer. I wasn't thinking of the people that were in front of me. I was thinking of the Lord, who was calling me at that moment. God gave me power when I prayed.

In the Bible, Psalm ninety-one is about getting in communion with God and staying away from evildoers. It says "you won't be fearful of the terror of the night, nor of the arrow that flies during the day; nor again the pest that is stalking in the shadows, nor the plague that destroys at noon. A thousand will fall on your left and ten thousand on your right. But nothing will touch you, or have an impact on you," or something like that. Those are beautiful passages.

❖ ❖

*He alone is my refuge, my place of safety;*
*he is my God, and I am trusting him. . . .*
*He will shelter [me] with his feathers. . . .*
*For he orders his angels*
*to protect [me] wherever [I] go.*
*They will hold [me] with their hands.*
—Psalm 91:2, 4, 11–12

*Melanio Ocampo Figuora*

# "I Would Pitch High and Outside"

## Jávier Gutierrez

*Jávier Gutierrez, eleven, is a shy fourth grader. Two years ago, when he was nine, Jávier fell out of a tree and scraped his right arm. It became infected down to the bone, and his arm had to be amputated because of the infection.*

*A year ago Jávier's mother, Gladys Cruz Gonzales, received a house through Rainbow's housing project. Before that she had lived with her husband who "left for another woman. Four kids were with me when he left."*

*Jávier says that in school he is studying "Spanish, science, civics, and mathematics. In science we are learning not to cut down trees and to take care of animals." When we get on the subject of baseball, Jávier comes to life. He wants to be a pitcher.*

> There is a baseball league here. I like to see them making runs and throwing the ball around and scoring. I like to play baseball. I have a strong throwing arm. I am good. As a pitcher you have to have control. My favorite pitch is a fastball. I would pitch high and outside. The most important person to the pitcher is the catcher. I would need a very good catcher.
>
> Jon said, "I'll be your catcher."

*The strong right arm of the LORD has done glorious things!*
*I will not die, but I will live.*

—Psalm 118:16–17

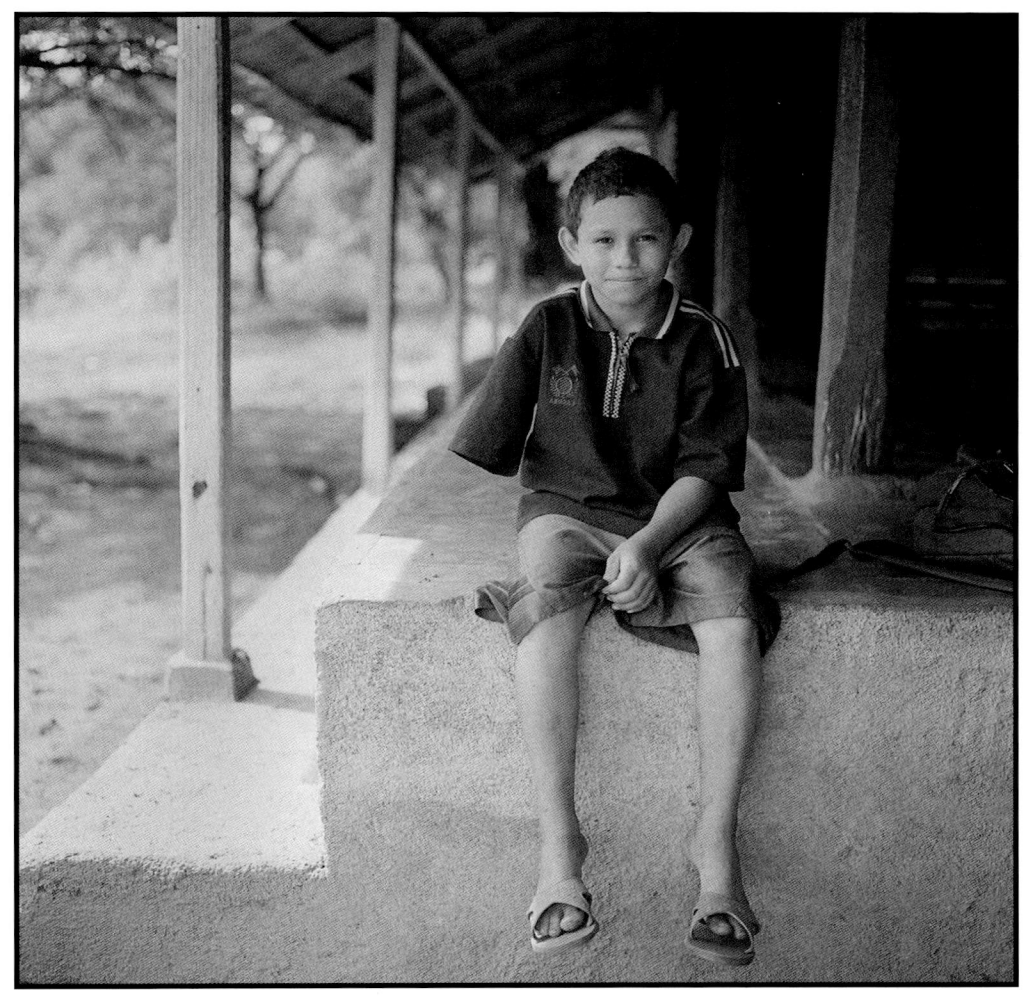

Jávier Gutierrez

# 11
# SAN RAMÓN

The farthest reaches of my travels lead Jon and me 120 miles north of Managua to the mountain community of San Ramón. Here lies an area of acute need, and here Rainbow established their most recent networks. The city center in this region is the one-time Sandinista stronghold of Matagalpa. Fierce battles took place here, and bullet holes can still be seen in the cracked, stucco siding of some buildings.

The beauty of mountains belies the desperate conditions of the inhabitants as well as the ghosts of their recent tragic history. Amid the beauty of palm trees, acacias, and mountain laurels, the people of San Ramón suffer in the extreme. Being so far removed from major city centers like Managua, and having been so hard hit from the civil war, the majority of its 16,000 residents do not have access to safe drinking water and other basic services and supplies. Children die on a regular basis because of malnutrition. Most people can't read or write. Keith said, "Everyone in this area is hungry all the time. There is someone sick in every household all the time."

Our escort for the day is Rainbow's director of education and the scholarship program in the region, a spirited, intelligent woman named Marilú Miranda Osegueda.

# "Spanish Is the Language of God"

## Marilú Miranda Osegueda

*In addition to serving as Rainbow's education director, Marilú Miranda Osegueda, thirty-eight, is a teacher of Spanish, a scholar and poet, and Rubén Darío expert par excellence. She has lived in San Ramón her entire life and has managed, through spirit and grit, to rise above its harsh circumstances. She attended university on Saturdays and took her degree in education. Rainbow recognized her gifts and hired her to oversee the educational needs of the neglected people in this mountainous region.*

I was nineteen, living in San Rafael del Norte during the war. It was a chilling situation. A lot of combat took place in that area. In my town, the Contras were fighting the Sandinistas and, unfortunately, I saw many, many people killed. I was traumatized by that situation. The shooting was all over the town. The Contras would take their bodies back with them, but the Sandinista bodies were scattered all over. Sometimes the Contras were unfair. They would come into town and if they didn't like you they would say, "You are a Sandinista" or "You are a friend of the Sandinistas," and then you die. Of course I was afraid in that situation. That psychologically affects you.

I am a poet from my nose to my mouth. Rubén Darío said, "The one who is not a romantic is better hung up from a pine tree." Spanish is a very rich language. It is richer to read a poem in Spanish than in English. Spanish is the language of God. English is the language of Clinton.

Of three prominent poets from Nicaragua, one was a crazy

*Marilú Miranda Osegueda*

writer, another was a priest, and another was a soldier. Our best poets were a soldier, a religious guy, and a crazy writer.

When people ask me where are you from? I tell them, "I come from a place where the wind comes late; where nobody is best or worst; I come from a place where everybody is equal." In the world there is no other nation as brave as my nation. I am a pure Nicaraguan *pinolero* [a typical drink made out of corn].

[She recited this poem]:

> *In a faraway nation a child-boy was born*
> *who later would become a good man*
> *with a heart full of love to others.*
> *He became a rich man and on a night*
> *with many stars in the sky, one star came down*
> *and whispered in his ear:*
> *Perhaps you can share your wealth*
> *with the poor children from a land of beautiful people*
> *who carry noble sentiments.*
> *That way, they, too, can give.*

Journalists have something of being a poet in them because of the writing. They want people to read. The words have to be beautiful to be attractive to people.

❖ ❖

*I will recite a lovely poem . . . ,*

*Put on your sword, O mighty warrior! . . .*

*Your arrows are sharp, . . .*

*Your throne, O God, endures forever and ever. . . .*

*Your robes are perfumed with myrrh. . . .*

*The bride, a princess, waits within her chamber,*

*dressed in a gown woven with gold.*

     —PSALM 45:1, 3, 5–6, 8, 13

## "God Made Me Brave"

### Alisa Alarcón

*Alisa Alarcón, an elderly woman of eighty, is great-grandmother of the baby she cares for (grandmother of the baby's father). The baby's name is Justo Pastor. For a long time he suffered from malnutrition and related maladies. Rainbow Network gave him the food and medical care he needed to survive. "We are very grateful," says the old woman. The baby's mother works in Managua and sends back money to support her four children*

I had twelve children of my own. Seven died. When my husband was alive he used to work and I could stay with the children. When he died we didn't have the same conditions.

I am able to walk. I can see. I can use my hands. I do laundry. I prepare beans and rice. I can't afford to have other things. You can look at the stove here. There is nothing else, only beans. The only thing is my feet get tired and my legs hurt.

I am eighty years old, but I am strong, *gracias a Diós*. God made me brave to take care of my grandson and great-grandchildren.

❖ ❖

He calmed the storm to a whisper. . . .
What a blessing was that stillness. . . .

—Psalm 107:29–30

*Alisa Alarcón*

# "I Feel Proud You Think of Me"

## José Alfredo Torres Mendez

*José Alfredo Torres Mendez, nineteen, wears an Indian's baseball cap. I ask if he is a fan of the Cleveland Indians and he doesn't know the team. He says he wears the cap to represent the indigenous heritage of the Nahuatl peoples, who once inhabited the region, and whose presence remains in evidence to this day. José Alfredo, the second of five siblings— two brothers and two sisters—is a Rainbow scholarship student in his second year, eighth grade.*

I want to have a better living standard in the future. Not the way I am living now. I am devoted completely to study and reviewing my lessons. Other days I go out to work. I work in agriculture, growing corn and beans. It depends on the rainy season whether we have a good or bad harvest. This season has been good. We are going to harvest some things.

I go to school on Saturdays from 8:00 to 3:45. I would like to be an engineer-agronomist. I do not have a girlfriend but, well, who knows? Maybe someday. I hope to get married and have a family once I get my education. It is hard for us to practice any sports. The two sports the people here like the most are baseball and soccer. We have a place here where we can play. But it is hard for us to get the equipment for us to play baseball and soccer.

I feel so proud as I know you think of me. I give thanks for such great love you have shown to all of us. I hope you are proud.

*José Alfredo Torres Mendez*

I prayerfully hope in God that he keeps you safe and may bless you always.

❖ ❖

*Your promises are backed*
*by all the honor of your name. . . .*
*You encourage me by giving me the*
   *strength I need. . . .*
*The glory of the LORD is very great.*
*Though the LORD is great, he cares for*
   *the humble.*
—Psalm 138:2–3, 5–6

# "I Ask My Creator to Give Me the Inspiration"

Abel Antonio García

*The first time I met Abel Antonio García, twenty, was in March 2003, during my previous trip to Nicaragua. Like José Alfredo, he too is a scholarship student sponsored by Rainbow, in his first year of high school, seventh grade. On that trip I saw him standing by his house, its sticks and mud serving as support for the plastic draped along the sides. Later we'd gathered in a school building where brightly splayed bougainvillea and cut flowers adorned the doorposts. The school was crammed with children, who sat at wood tables holding papers and pencils, lifting their drawings for us to see. Someone said, "The children are very happy because they have been waiting for you."*

*An older student stepped from the crowd and lifted a paper. Someone said, "He's written a poem. He is going to read it." It was the same young man I'd seen earlier standing beside the mud house. His eyes were dark and narrow, with a glint that showed him to be a poet. "You've been here for eight months"—he projected well—"I give thanks to God because you have been here forever. . . . The day you came my heart blossomed, I had new breath in my life. I have come back to life again. . . ."*

*Later, as our group took our leave, I found that young man. "You are a very good poet," I said. "What is your name?" He said, "My name is Abel Antonio García." I said, "That is a good name for a Nicaraguan poet." Our group prepared to reboard the van and Abel followed us. As he stood by the roadside to say good-bye, I shook his hand. "Keep writing poetry," I said. "Here is my pen."*

*He took it between his fingers. I looked back and saw him standing there on the rocky path in that impoverished mountain village, his hair neatly combed and his smile so poised, I regretted having given him a pen with so little ink left in it. I thought,* What will he use to write poetry with when that little bit of ink is gone?

*When I return with Jon in July, I bring Abel more pens. He speaks of what inspires him.*

I'm inspired from the bottom of my heart, by the love and affection you people from the United States, and also Rainbow, have brought to me and my community, especially the children. From the inspiration, words come, and I write them down for you because of the love you have shown.

We are eight—six sisters and one brother. I am the oldest. My father passed away, so my mother is a widow. She is raising us by herself. I love my sisters and the only brother I have. I also love my mother. I make many efforts to thank Rainbow for supporting my schooling. I'm going to study hard and, God willing, in the future I am going to support my younger brother and sisters. They need to keep going forward.

I believe in God. God has given me a lot. I believe that you are a blessing from God and that Rainbow has come to our community where there is so much need. I always pray to God for my health situation, for my schooling, for you and for your family, and for Rainbow. God is my savior and my helper. Whenever I write a poem, I ask my creator first to give me the intelligence and inspiration to write it.

Sometimes I get sick all of a sudden. It's not that we have very serious health problems. But we have some problems. All of the children in my community are malnourished. All of them are very poor. The children are very thin, very short. Their parents are unemployed. It is a hard economic situation. There is no way to give them food. When you see them they are in bad condition. It shouldn't be the way a boy develops. Thanks to Rainbow we

Abel Antonio García

have the opportunity to provide for them. We hope and pray to God that God will bless you.

We are very happy and grateful to you for your visit to my community. I feel as though you are my mother and Jon is one of my brothers. Now that I have Jon as one of my brothers, he will be very close to my heart. From my affection I would like that you would stay here forever. I don't like that you have to leave. I'd like to have you here always with me. I pray to God every day for you and hold you in my heart. We are waiting for you here. I have written this poem with much love:

> *What can I tell you*
> *Now that you are present in my heart*
> *Living always a hope?*
> *I send you kisses, for you have always been,*
> *After God, my earthly princess,*
> *The guardian angel that watches over me.*
> *You give me everlasting affection and love.*
> *You are the air that I breathe.*

❖  ❖

*My heart overflows with a beautiful thought! . . .*

*for my tongue is like the pen of a skillful poet. . . .*

*Gracious words stream from your lips.*

*God himself has blessed you forever.*

—PSALM 45:1–2

# CONCLUSION

I have never in all my life been called the air someone breathed. I knew when Abel spoke those words, he was not speaking of me so much as what it feels like when someone brings hope. I'd asked myself many times through the writing of this book, *Why me? Who am I to be writing about these people's lives and how God answered their prayers and made dreams come true?* For a long time I'd thought I was writing a book about an ordinary man with extraordinary instincts who had a big wallet and a heart for the poor. I thought I was writing a book about what one person can do who grabs a vision, pokes a hole in it, and steps inside. I was. But I have come to understand that I have been writing about more than that.

At the beginning of that second trip, Jon and I, with our traveling companions Tim and Ali Geisse, and Ali's friend Caroline, were reposing in the shade at the base of Volcán Mombacho. Unlike the smoking Volcán Masaya, this one is extinct, its cavity overgrown with lush jungle. We were awaiting a "bus" (a war-beaten army truck with a gun turret in the roof) to take us to the top of the mountain where we'd hike the lip of the volcano. Waiting for the bus, Ali, Caroline, and I started to chat about their love of singing, both of them with voices clear and gentle as wind chimes. "Let's sing," I said. They hesitated, not wanting to draw attention to themselves. "You'll bless people," I said. So they sang: *The Lord bless you and keep you, the Lord raise his countenance upon you and give you peace; the Lord make his face to shine upon you and be gracious unto you.* Then we caught the bus to the top of the mountain.

Skies had been blue and the sun hot at the base of the mountain. It never occurred to us to bring our rain gear, tucked dutifully in the back of our truck. At the top, however, once on the trail deep inside the jungle canopy, it began to rain. Then it poured. We sought refuge under trees. Eventually, deeming it hopeless, we surrendered to the elements and received baptism by immersion in a mid-summer storm.

We came upon a fork in the path and felt sure bearing right would lead us to the shelter and warmth of the park station. In a spontaneous flourish of abandon—drenched as we were—Jon, Caroline, and I decided, what the heck, let's go left and see where it takes us. The trails in puddles, our shoes like soaked sponges, we walked and walked beneath the dripping trees, chilled and our spirit of adventure fading.

Then the forest gave way to a grassy ridge. We stood overlooking a view of the city of Granada and the archipelago of isles off its eastern shore in Lake Cociloka, formed when Mombacho blew thousands of years before. We followed a muddy path to a nook where, oddly, we felt warmth arising from the earth. Chilled and wet, we followed the warmth until we came to a spot where steam rose from rocks off the path. The three of us huddled around the rising warmth, a gift freely given from the bowels of the mountain. When we returned to the path, the sun had broken through a low cloud. Stunning streaks of light luminesced a billowing cloud over the hillside where we stood. A gentle wind stirred. Steam rose beneath our feet. In that moment the forces of heaven and earth came together, from below and above, and showed themselves in harmony. That, I came to see, is really what this story is about.

It is about a kind man, his instincts, his heart, his generous wallet—and the kind hearts and generous wallets of other people. It is a book about the work of an "NGO."

It is a book about wars, and damage, and survival, and dreams; like a bird singing a song on a knobby tree at the edge of a belching volcano.

It is about how little it takes to bring someone hope; about the transaction that takes place when, poverty-stricken in spirit, a person begins to think like God and becomes meek before God, and hungers and thirsts for the right thing.

It is about a Springfield millionaire who dons a baseball cap and slogs through the mountains looking for a place to build. It is about a lawyer in a Piggly-Wiggly T-shirt fixing shelves and perfecting camera angles. It is about a man in a wheelchair, a baby on his lap, who lost use of his legs on the road to bury his sister, and yet says thanks to God "who is big." It is about the silence that fell when the Chessies locked up and Keith mounted a table to get them on track. It is about

Mel and Charlene and Tom and Bob and others in that boardroom laboring hours over how to build a good house in the mountains of San Ramón. It is about David Ubeda's shining eyes, though he carried a gun at the age of twelve. It is about Maritza Solarzano's beans on the fire and her birth certificate that enabled her to believe she was not an animal; that she existed. It is about little Juana Santana's need to say "thank you" for her doll, and her dreams about "a tall guy and handsome and in a nice mood." It is about Ericka Acuña, who's gentle and brave and at peace with herself as she bears in her fragile frame the burdens of the women of her country. It's about Aleyda Hernandez who helps neighbors in God's name, despite memories of neighbors being killed for helping neighbors. It's about Marilú Osegueda reading her poem on a roadside in the most beautiful language in the world. It's about her word to me, "journalists have something of a poet in them" too. It's about Carlos Reál, the ten-year-old whose heart broke into verse when his mother went away, and his dreams of being a goalie, who might perhaps control the losses. It's about Jávier Gutierrez, the little tree-climber who lost an arm for want of ointment, who'd pitch high and outside with an able catcher. It's about dear Marcos, my translator and friend whose heart broke with mine, recounting the suffering of his people. His own life has seen grief enough to break the strongest of men. He called me a gorilla, *ja ja*. Our laughter gave us strength. It's about Abel Antonio García, the Nicaraguan poet who called me "the air he breathed." It's about a journalist who gave away her pen.

Our souls lean on each other. I saw the sun pour light over a cold wet earth. I felt rain and winds and wet shoes that finally led to warmth freely given from cracks in the earth. I heard a song in these voices, like a blessing sung at the base of a mountain. I've called this a story of rebirth, a tale of revolution and dreams, of betrayal and new hope, about being lost and found.

How little it takes to bring someone hope. The sun broke, beauty arose, mud led to warmth and the sky opened. Heaven meets earth when our souls greet each other. O God, you made us all so wonderfully. May your light fall on us and may we give it back, and share your beauty and hear your song arise in benediction from the people in the land of smoking mountains.

*The author confers with her warrior translator.*

# ENDNOTES

1. Rubén Darío, "Poets! Towers of God," in Eleven Poems of Rubén Darío, trans. Salomón de la Selva (New York and London: G. P. Putnam's Sons, 1916). The original Spanish title "Torres de Dios Poetas!" reads:

    *Torres de Dios Poetas!*
    *Pararrayos celestes,*
    *que resistís las duras tempestades,*
    *como crestas escuetas,*
    *como picos agrestes,*
    *rompeolas de las eternidades!*
    *La mágica Esperanza anuncia el día*
    *en que sobre la roca de armonía*
    *expirar la pérfida sirena.*
    *Esperad, esperemos todavía!*

## INTRODUCTION
1. Written by Abel Antonio García, Las Rosas, San Ramón; © Abel Antonio García, 2003.

## CHAPTER 1
1. George A. Buttrick, *Prayer* (Nashville: Abingdon, 1942), 56.

## CHAPTER 2
1. Eduardo del Rio (Ruís), *Nicaragua for Beginners* (New York: Writers and Readers Publishing, 1984), 12.
2. In Latin America the "liberal party" is equivalent to the conservative party in the U.S.; my denotation here retains associations North Americans would bring to these terms, in contradistinction to their associations in Nicaragua.
3. Quoted in Stephen Kinzer, *Blood of Brothers* (New York: G. P. Putnam's Sons, 1991), 27.
4. Ibid., 28.

## CHAPTER 3
1. Quoted in Stephen Kinzer, *Blood of Brothers* (New York: G. P. Putnam's Sons, 1991), 375.

For information about partnering
with Rainbow Network, please contact:

Keith Jaspers, President
Rainbow Network
3834 South Ave., Springfield, MO 65807
Voice 417-889-8088 ❖ Fax 417-889-3815

In Nicaragua, Rainbow Network is known as *Red Arco Iris*,
which is Spanish for Rainbow Network.

---

## RAINBOW NETWORK
### BOARD OF DIRECTORS
### 2005

Rocky Levell, Chair
*Springfield, Missouri*

Keith Jaspers, President
*Springfield, Missouri*

Romona Baker, Secretary
*Willard, Missouri*

Dr. Robert Carolla
*Springfield, Missouri*

Tim Geisse
*Chagrin Falls, Ohio*

Dr. Roger Ray
*Springfield, Missouri*

Phil Stocker
*Springfield, Missouri*

Betty Baldner, Vice-Chair
*La Crosse, Wisconsin*

Karen Jaspers, Treasurer
*Springfield, Missouri*

Tom Cardin
*Springfield, Missouri*

Rev. Bruce Davis
*Springfield, Missouri*

Charlene Meyer
*Cincinnati, Ohio*

Dr. Ed Schanda
*Forsyth, Missouri*

Rev. Mel West
*Columbia, Missouri*